LET JUSTICE BE DONE

LET JUSTICE BE DONE

Writings from American Abolitionists
1688–1865

Kerry Walters, editor

ORBIS BOOKS

Maryknoll, New York 10545

ORBIS BOOKS
Maryknoll, New York 10545

Fathers and Brothers
MARYKNOLL

Founded in 1970, Orbis Books endeavors to publish works that enlighten the mind, nourish the spirit, and challenge the conscience. The publishing arm of the Maryknoll Fathers and Brothers, Orbis seeks to explore the global dimensions of the Christian faith and mission, to invite dialogue with diverse cultures and religious traditions, and to serve the cause of reconciliation and peace. The books published reflect the views of their authors and do not represent the official position of the Maryknoll Society. To learn more about Maryknoll and Orbis Books, please visit our website at www.orbisbooks.com

Manufactured in the United States of America

Library of Congress Cataloging-in-Publication Data

On file with publisher.

Contents

PART TWO
The Early Republic:
Terrible in Crime and Magnitude

PART THREE
The Antebellum Period:
Christ vs. the Slavocracy

L'ENVOY

PREFACE

I am an Abolitionist!
Oppression's deadly foe;
In God's great strength will I resist,
And lay the monster low.
            —William Lloyd Garrison

Beginning toward the end of the seventeenth century and continuing until the end of the antebellum period, a prophetic crusade to eliminate the sin of slavery stirred the American conscience, inspiring some to wholehearted dedication to the cause and inciting others to furious resistance to it. Eventually, around the 1830s, the movement came to be called abolitionism.

Almost to a person, the abolitionists were deeply faithful Christians who believed that if anything was contrary to the will of God, it was human bondage. For five generations, in lectures, sermons, books, newspapers, and public demonstrations that became increasingly numerous and more zealous with each passing decade, they doggedly denounced it. Their numbers were never large, but their impact was profound. Thanks to the abolitionists' fervor and perseverance, people in both the North and South who may never have questioned the moral legitimacy of slavery, much less reflected on its incompatibility with Christian commitment, could no longer claim ignorance of its horrors. Even though there's no hard data, it's more than likely that the abolitionists' tireless condemnation of slavery converted a good number of people to their way of thinking. Prophets, even if reviled in the short run, often do succeed in touching hearts and changing minds.

The anti-slavery crusade was the first intentional interracial collaboration in the United States, comparable in that respect to the twentieth century's civil rights movement. Like that later campaign, it was based on biblical principles of human dignity, the right to freedom, and duty to God. Also like the civil rights movement, the abolitionist crusade frequently likened its struggle to the Exodus story of Moses leading the Hebrews out of Egyptian bondage.

The abolitionist struggle against one of the greatest evils to blemish American history demonstrated that religious faith can and rightfully should be a powerful force in calling out injustice, speaking truth to power, and influencing public opinion and policy for the better. These days, when Christianity in America is rocked by scandal, hijacked by ideologues, and distrusted—if not downright despised—by significant numbers of people, it's good to be reminded of what it once was and what it can be again. My hope is that the writings collected here will inspire Christians today to remember who we are and what we're capable of.

———

The selections in this anthology are only a small but, I trust, representative sample of American anti-slavery writings. Except for correcting typographical errors in the original texts, I've retained original spellings, punctuation, and even (in most cases) infelicitous grammar.

The abolitionists quoted scripture liberally, but usually without attribution; Christians were much more conversant with the Bible in those days than we are in ours, so I've supplied bracketed chapter and verse references when there are none in the original. The handful of footnotes are mine, as are all the ellipses, meant to indicate editorial breaks in the selections.

Readers wishing to explore American abolitionism in more detail may find the bibliography that concludes this volume useful.

Introduction

Let Justice Be Done though the Heavens May Fall

The New England poet John Greenleaf Whittier, Quaker and passionate opponent of slavery, awoke on the morning of January 31, 1865, to the sound of pealing bells. It signaled the ratification of the Thirteenth Amendment, which ended slavery in the United States once and for all.

Like so many other Americans who deplored the "peculiar institution," as proslavery senator from South Carolina John C. Calhoun affirmingly dubbed it, Whittier had been agitating for years for an end to the legalized reduction of black persons to livestock. When the day of slavery's dissolution finally arrived, he marked the joyous occasion by composing a poem, "Laus Deo," in which he said that he "heard God's own voice" in the peals and then triumphantly proclaimed,

> When was ever His right hand
> Over any time or land
> Stretched as now beneath the sun!

It was customary in Whittier's time, as it is in ours, to invoke God's name in public announcements of great events. It can scarcely be doubted that doing so, especially today, is sometimes little more than a *de rigueur* but noncommittal nod to religious sensibility intended to add a bit of heft to the occasion. But when Whittier and the vast majority of his fellow abolitionists appealed to God, they were perfectly earnest, convinced as they were that slavery was an abomination in the eyes of the Creator and that struggling against it was a Christian moral duty ignored—or, even worse, resisted—at great spiritual cost. American abolitionism, beginning with its earliest public expressions in the late seventeenth century and continuing right through to the ratification of the Thirteenth Amendment, was a primarily Christian crusade aimed at eradicating a great evil. The movement counted in its ranks women and men, blacks and whites, and church-going as well as "come-outer" Christians—those who, out of disgust for their denominations' refusal to condemn slavery, walked away from church membership.

Some abolitionists actively aided runaway slaves by serving as conductors or stationmasters on the Underground Railroad, the maze of secret trails followed by fugitive slaves. Others contributed funds and supplies to build up the movement. Still others drew the general public's attention to the horrors of slavery through essays, books, poetry, song, lectures, sermons, and journalistic articles and cartoons.

All of them risked public scorn, imprisonment, and even, at times, physical danger. William Lloyd Garrison, for example, was nearly lynched by a proslavery mob in Boston. Elijah Lovejoy, a Presbyterian minister and publisher of an antislavery journal, was murdered for his stance. Harriet Tubman, the "Moses of her people," the ex-slave who returned to the South again and again to guide her men and women from bondage to freedom, had dead-or-alive bounties placed on her head by furious slave owners. Yet they all persevered, convinced that their fidelity to Christ gave them no other choice than to risk much and perhaps all to put an end to slavery. This, they accepted, was the time in which God had placed them and the task he had given them.

American Slavery

The Jamestown colony in what is modern-day Virginia had been in existence for only twelve years when the *Jesus of Lubeck*, a

Dutch ship, landed there in 1619 and traded nineteen African captives for badly needed supplies. So far as we know, these were the earliest arrivals to the North American shore of Africans transported against their will.

The Jamestown Africans were treated as indentured servants and eventually freed, probably after they'd worked off the value of the commodities traded for them, and given land of their own. But by mid-century, what had begun as black indentured labor in the colonies of Virginia and Maryland had been transformed into lifelong coerced servitude, a condition usually called "chattel slavery." Slaves—a term that became synonymous with persons of color who couldn't prove their freedom—were legally forbidden to own property. They had no legal standing in court, couldn't engage in business or civic activities, couldn't marry legally or travel without permits, and were subject to routine physical abuse. The children of slave mothers were automatically born into slavery. They, and all other slaves, could be sold at their owner's will. And unless they were freed for one reason or another by a legal writ of manumission, they would die in slavery. Perhaps inevitably, the assumption that blacks were inferior to whites, and hence good only as slaves, also became widespread. It's difficult and probably impossible to determine the causal relationship between North American slavery and racism. But it's beyond dispute that the one served as a legitimation of the other.

Slaves, in other words, were the absolute property or chattel of their owners, a condition that reduced them to what historian James Oakes called "permanent outsiders" whose very humanity had been stolen from them.[1] Many ex-slaves testified to this horrible loss of identity. One of them, John Parker, a fugitive who became a key figure in the Ohio Underground Railroad, put it like

---

1. James Oakes, *Slavery and Freedom: An Interpretation of the Old South* (New York: Alfred K. Knopf, 1990), chapter 1.

this: "It was not the physical part of slavery that made it cruel and degrading, it was the taking away from a human being the initiative, of thinking, of doing his own ways. Slavery's curse was not pain of the body, but the pain of the soul."[2]

The Revolutionary War's Enlightenment ideals of liberty and equality invited a reconsideration of the moral propriety of slavery and its consistency with the stated values of the young Republic. Northern state legislatures began eliminating slavery within their borders, Vermont first in 1777, followed by Massachusetts/Maine (one state at the time), New Hampshire, Pennsylvania, Connecticut, Rhode Island, New York, and finally, in 1804, New Jersey. Congress banned the importation of slaves into the United States after 1808, and the 1787 Northwest Ordinance forbade the spread of slavery in the vast stretch of land—modern-day Illinois, Indiana, Michigan, Ohio, and Wisconsin—ceded by England after the War of Independence.

During this period, even the slave-heavy southern states began rethinking the value of the peculiar institution, not so much out of moral concerns as of economic interests. Sugar and cotton crops in the Lower South were so labor intensive that farmers who grew them tended to plant and harvest modestly, and so needed only moderate slave labor. As arable land in the Upper South lost its vitality through overplanting of cash crops like tobacco, slave labor in Maryland and Virginia became less essential, and thousands of slaves were manumitted by owners unwilling to shoulder the financial burden of keeping them, especially after they had grown old and were no longer able to work. The numbers of freed slaves swelled so alarmingly that several early Republic leaders formed the American Colonization Society in 1816 with the express purpose of transporting freedmen to Africa, despite the fact that a progressively enlarg-

---

2. John Parker, *His Promised Land: The Autobiography of John P. Parker,* ed. Stuart Seely Sprague (New York: W. W. Norton, 1996), 25, 26.

ing percentage of them had been born and raised in North America. The Society would be excoriated by abolitionists as a racist-fueled engine of exile masquerading as a humanitarian effort.

The course of slavery changed abruptly in 1792 with Eli Whitney's invention of the cotton gin, a remarkably simple device that enabled the rapid carding of seed from raw cotton. Before its appearance, it took about ten hours for a slave to clean a single pound of cotton. With the gin, upwards of one thousand pounds could be carded in a day. Almost overnight, cotton production in the South boomed. Farms became plantations as enterprising southerners bought up huge tracts of land to raise more and more cotton, and this, of course, increased the market demand for slave labor. Just four years after Whitney's gin revolutionized the industry, the South was exporting upwards of two million pounds of cotton. By the mid-nineteenth century, annual production topped a million tons, and the number of slaves had mushroomed to around four million, 18 percent of the nation's total population. As South Carolina senator James Hammond frankly said, "Cotton is King, and the African must be slave, or there's an end of all things, and soon."[3]

Cotton, which quickly became the United States' chief export, boosted the economy of the entire nation. Northern manufacturers processed cotton into cloth, and retailers sold the products made from it. Upper South slave states profited from selling slaves to Lower South slave states, especially after the 1808 deadline on slave importations kicked in. As a consequence, most whites, who already believed in the inferiority of African slaves, accepted slavery as an economic necessity, even if it pricked their consciences. Many would have agreed with Thomas Jefferson's observation that slavery is "the most unremitting despotism on the one part, and degrading submissions on the

---

3. Ronald G. Walters, *American Reformers, 1815-1860* (New York: Hill and Wang, 1978), 78.

other," even if they might not have been as brutally frank.[4] But like Jefferson, himself a lifelong slave owner, most Americans both tolerated and materially benefited from human bondage.

EARLY ANTI-SLAVERY SENTIMENTS

Most, but not all Americans tolerated slavery. Beginning as early as the late seventeenth century, a few voices began calling out slavery for the moral outrage that it was, and doing so from explicitly Christian perspectives.

The first public protests came for the most part from members of the Society of Friends, or Quakers. The sect's founder, George Fox, had taught that "tawnies and blacks" were saved by Christ's sacrifice just as much as whites, and that they should be treated accordingly. But this didn't inhibit many of his American co-religionists from owning and trading in human chattel.

In 1688, several Germantown, Pennsylvania, Mennonites-turned-Quakers challenged their slaveholding brethren by issuing the first public anti-slavery statement in the British colonies. They argued that "traffick of mens-body" amounted to theft, adultery, and violence, none of which were compatible with Quaker principles. Their protest was received and promptly buried by the Philadelphia Yearly Meeting. But their cause was taken up a generation later by an itinerant and eccentric Quaker preacher named Benjamin Lay, and after him by the better-remembered John Woolman, who insisted that mistreating others by keeping them as slaves dimmed the Inner Light with which all persons were born. The anti-slavery campaign on the part of these Quakers eventually bore fruit. Ninety years after the Germantown protest, Quaker Meetings throughout New England, Pennsylvania, and Virginia finally disowned the practice of slavery and threatened with expulsion members who persisted in owning or selling slaves.

---

4. Thomas Jefferson, *Notes on the State of Virginia*, in *The Writings of Thomas Jefferson*, ed. Paul Leicester Ford (New York: G. P. Putnam's Sons, 1905), IV:300.

Quakers in the colonial and early Republic eras weren't the only Christians to resist slavery. Although Catholic voices then and later were mainly mute about the immorality of slavery, Protestants such as Congregationalist Samuel Sewall and Presbyterian Theodore Dwight joined Quakers in their condemnation of it. Equally if not more important were the denunciations from persons of color that began to appear. One year before the eruption of the War of Independence, black poet Phyllis Wheatley published an open letter denouncing the "strange Absurdity of Conduct" displayed by persons who professed to love Christ while owning human beings. David Walker, a free black Baltimorean, argued in an 1829 book that slaves had a moral right to resort to arms if doing so was the only way to break free of their chains.

The Abolitionist Crusade

The earliest Christian objections to slavery in North America, even those coming from Quakers, tended to be individual and sporadic. But condemnation of the peculiar institution began to coalesce into an organized movement by the early 1830s.

Whereas earlier denunciations of slavery typically had called for the gradual and compensated emancipation of slaves, this new generation of activists more radically insisted on immediate and uncompensated abolition. Why, they demanded, should the moral blight of slavery be permitted to continue for even a day longer? And why ought men and women who owned slaves be rewarded for their sin? For this new generation of abolitionists, slavery was the nation's central and overwhelming sin, the one that spawned any number of others such as theft, greed, adultery, and cruelty. Therefore, it had to be ended immediately and completely. Although himself a gradualist, abolitionist Benjamin Lundy captured the urgency felt by antebellum opponents of slavery when he proclaimed in the masthead of his newspaper *Genius of Universal Emancipation*, "Let Justice Be Done Though the Heavens May Fall!"

Much of the fervor that the new abolitionists brought to their campaign against slavery can be attributed to the enthusiasm for large-scale moral reform precipitated by what came to be known as the Second Great Awakening, a largely Protestant revivalist movement that began at the end of the eighteenth century and peaked in the early 1840s. (The First Great Awakening revival, especially associated with figures like George Whitefield and Jonathan Edwards, had occurred a century earlier.) The Second Awakening called for a renewal among Christians in regard to the spiritual states of their souls and their moral role as citizens. The first demanded personal repentance and conversion, the second a thoroughgoing reformation of society to eradicate social injustice and ungodly opportunities for sin. Accordingly, an entire spectrum of reformist movements—having to do with temperance, humane treatment of the mentally ill and the imprisoned, improvement of education, securing of women's rights, abolition of capital punishment, and even advocacy of a vegetarian diet—became popular. Proponents of the abolition of slavery were energized by the revivalists' reformist agenda, and eventually proved to be some of its most vocal and organized prophets.

Without doubt, the most influential white leader in this new wave of anti-slavery was William Lloyd Garrison, a one-time colonizationist and gradualist who grew so disgusted with slavery— a practice, he wrote, that made "angels weep"—that he launched the abolitionist newspaper *Liberator* on January 1, 1831, to agitate for immediate emancipation. His opening editorial was a bombshell that rallied fellow abolitionists and outraged slave owners and defenders of slavery.

> I am aware that many object to the severity of my language; but is there not cause for severity? I will be as harsh as truth, and as uncompromising as justice. On this subject, I do not wish to think, or to speak, or write, with moderation. No! no! Tell a man whose house is on fire to give a moderate alarm; tell him to moderately rescue his

wife from the hands of the ravisher; tell the mother to gradually extricate her babe from the fire into which it has fallen; but urge me not to use moderation in a cause like the present. I am in earnest—I will not equivocate—I will not excuse—I will not retreat a single inch—AND I WILL BE HEARD.

The *Liberator* became the movement's leading organ for the next thirty-five years before printing its final issue in 1865. Enjoying the widest readership of any of the many abolitionist publications that sprang up in the antebellum period, the *Liberator* gave black and white opponents of slavery a powerful and widely read platform from which to defend their cause. As a consequence, many of these people became household names. The Grimké sisters, Theodore Dwight Weld, Sojourner Truth, Frederick Douglass, Henry Highland Garnet, Lucretia Mott, Harriet Beecher Stowe, and of course Garrison himself all regularly contributed to the newspaper's pages.

Garrison and his fellow anti-slavery agitators recognized that the success of their campaign depended upon organized coordination. In 1832, they founded the New England Anti-Slavery Society in Boston. Financed in large part by Arthur and Lewis Tappan, evangelical brothers who had made fortunes in business, the Society expressly welcomed black members to its ranks, something of an innovation at the time. The following year, abolitionism's growing popularity led to the founding of a national organization, the American Anti-Slavery Society (AAS). Its Declaration of Sentiments, largely written by Garrison, became a manifesto of sorts for the entire movement. Internal dissent within the Society, primarily over the role of women but also having to do with politics, would later lead to defections, most notably that of the Tappan brothers. But the AAS remained a strong force and spawned dozens of local abolitionist subsidiaries.

Members of the AAS, often and somewhat misleadingly called Garrisonians, believed that the proper weapon to use against slavery was what they called "moral suasion": moral and religious appeals to the consciences of southern slave owners and northern defenders of slavery. AAS members embraced a policy of nonviolence, although in a sometimes inconsistently hit-and-miss way. Garrison himself, for example, while not exactly advocating armed slave uprisings, refused to condemn them. Others, like Thomas Wentworth Higginson, actually served as a combat soldier in the Civil War. Still other abolitionists supported, even if only reluctantly, the war effort.

As the years passed and slavery remained intact, Garrisonians came to believe that Congress's refusal to outlaw slavery in the southern states revealed the government's utter moral corruption (to express his contempt, Garrison once publicly burned a copy of the Constitution) and they eschewed all involvement in electoral politics, even in the abolitionist Liberty Party that flourished for a short while in the 1840s. This position eventually led to a break between Garrison and Frederick Douglass, the leading black abolitionist of his day. Disdain was also directed at mainline Christian denominations that refused to condemn slavery or excommunicate slavery-approving members. For Garrisonian abolitionists, such churches were as fallen as the government.

One of the most distinctive convictions of the abolitionists, Garrisonian or otherwise—as well as being the cause of much angry resistance to them—was their view that the black and white races were, in God's eyes, equally deserving of respect and moral consideration. Any intellectual or moral weakness displayed by slaves was the result of cultural conditioning rather than nature, and to believe otherwise was sheer prejudice. In hindsight, it's clear that the abolitionists themselves weren't immune from the prejudice they decried. They could be paternalistic and condescending in their collaboration with free blacks and quite hopelessly out of their depth when it came to relating to exslaves who were illiterate and uncultured. But their insistence on Christian egalitarian principles, even if they didn't always honor them, was a mainstay of the movement.

Not all abolitionists adopted the Garrisonian strategy of moral suasion. By the 1850s, when a repressive law known as the Fugitive Slave Act made even free states unsafe for runaway slaves and the Dred Scott Supreme Court decision stripped all blacks of constitutional rights, it became clear to abolitionist activists like ex-slaves Frederick Douglass and Henry Highland Garnet that the only effective route to emancipation was armed revolt. Both of them approved of the fiery prophet John Brown's raid on the federal arsenal at Harpers Ferry in October 1859, which Brown hoped would spark a general insurrection among Virginia and Maryland slaves. When it ingloriously failed, Brown, convinced to the end that he'd been commissioned by God to lead slaves to freedom, was hanged. Although viewed by most Americans as a frightening zealot, he became a martyr and hero to the abolitionists.

That the abolitionists for the most part based their crusade on their Christian faith and the principles of morality did not go unnoticed by their opponents in both the North and South who frequently responded to them in kind. Defenders of slavery, ordained as well as lay, insisted that there was no scriptural condemnation of slavery. Even more, they often invoked Paul's Letter to Philemon as an express justification of it. Stretching scripture to the breaking point, they argued against racial equality by insisting that blacks were the result of a separate act of divine creation and hence not from the same stock as whites or, alternatively, that persons of color were the cursed descendants of Ham and specifically doomed to be subordinate to whites. They also justified the peculiar institution by claiming that the enslavement of Africans was actually in their best spiritual and moral interest because it exposed them to the saving doctrines of Christianity of which they would have otherwise remained ignorant. And, for good measure, they asserted that slaves were treated far more humanely by paternalistic southern masters than free wage laborers were by their money-grubbing northern employers.

A typical example of the many Christian rebuttals of abolitionism was the Reverend Ebenezer Warren's novel *Nellie Norton; or Southern Slavery and the Bible*. Explicitly advertising itself
as a "A Scriptural Refutation of the Principal Arguments Upon
Which the Abolitionists Rely," the book was obviously inspired
by Harriet Beecher Stowe's bestselling *Uncle Tom's Cabin*. In
Warren's story, Nellie, a young woman returning to her "Southern soil and home" after a few years in a New England finishing
school, has been more or less brainwashed by her sojourn in the
North and has to be reeducated about the many virtues of slavery.
In the tediously stilted dialogue that was all too common in bad
nineteenth-century literature, Nellie is systematically purged of
the northern criticisms of slavery she imbibed and providentially
tutored in what Rev. Warren sees as the truth about slavery: that
slaves actually prefer it to freedom, that it's scripturally war-
ranted, and that to oppose it—not to mention seeking to abolish
it—is to upset the natural order of things by interfering with the
divine plan.

Difficult as it may be to comprehend today when the immorality of slavery seems so painfully obvious to nearly everyone, religious disagreements over slavery and emancipation tore
apart Christian families as well as entire denominations in the
antebellum period. The Baptists, Methodists, and Presbyterians
all split over it, and abolitionists were quick to condemn fellow
Christians who refused to repent of their defense of slavery or
who sanctioned its horrors by their silence. In addition to criti-
cizing churches, abolitionists blasted the American Tract Society and the American Bible Society for their failure to denounce
the peculiar institution as antithetical to Christianity. Ex-slave
and abolitionist William Wells Brown mordantly pointed out
that the American Tract Society believed it a Christian duty to
issue pamphlets on the "sin" of dancing but utterly ignored the
far graver one of slavery.

By the time the Civil War erupted in 1861, the fault line between Christians who supported and Christians who opposed

human bondage had become unbridgeable and peaceful coexistence impossible. It's no exaggeration to say that each camp considered the other to be the Antichrist, each misusing the Bible for its own purposes, each distorting the faith to further an unholy cause, each unjustly condemning the other. The key difference, however, is that one side was objectively right, and the other objectively wrong.

The Case for Abolition

Although there were differences in methods endorsed by Christian opponents of slavery—gradual versus immediate emancipation, moral suasion versus armed resistance, and moral suasion versus political action—there was near unanimity among them when it came to spelling out the Christian case against slavery and for abolition.

As already noted, the abolitionists believed that all humans, regardless of their skin color, share the same essential nature by virtue of their common origin. Each and every person made in the image of God was seen as having been endowed with an identity that conferred upon him or her certain natural rights which simply couldn't be gainsaid without defying God's will. One of these natural rights was freedom. In its absence, humans—first the enslaved, but eventually the enslavers as well—are unable to flourish. Slaves suffer dehumanization—as Theodore Dwight Weld grippingly put it, slavery "unseats a man to make room for a thing"—and enslavers sink into the quagmire of moral corruption and religious hypocrisy.

The abolitionists also saw slavery as a totalizing embodiment of sin. There wasn't, in their estimation, a single one of the Ten Commandments left unviolated by the practice of chattel slavery. Consequently, as William Lloyd Garrison proclaimed, it was the "embodiment of all criminality." Ripping Africans apart from their families or selling domestic slaves away from theirs was the cruelest form of theft. The sexual abuse of slaves by unscrupulous masters was both a crime against their victims and an adulterous betrayal of their wives. Placing wealth in slaves ahead of obedience to God's will as expressed through the teachings of Christ was idolatry. Reducing creatures made in the image of God to the moral and spiritual status of soulless objects or dumb beasts of burden was murder. And so on.

Moreover, slavery encouraged a sin that was unknown to the ancient Hebrews and hence unspecified in the Decalogue but that the abolitionists saw as a particularly grave offense against both God and morality: the racist view that blacks were inferior to whites and hence properly destined to live subservient existences. Garrison coined an expressive word for this attitude. He called it "colorphobia": an aversion to persons of color so intense that it stifled both empathy and common human decency when it came to dealing with such persons.

Just as pervasively, slavery was a catalyst for mendacity and cowardice in both individuals and society at large. In order to justify the peculiar institution, its defenders had to ignore or distort facts, even to the point of blasphemy. Sometimes they resorted to outright mendacity, but more often than not they were the victims of self-deception and rationalization. Slaveholders often twisted scripture to legitimize their treatment of blacks by claiming that God had ordained slavery and falsely asserting that slaves were actually happier in bondage than they otherwise would be, or insisting that a free wage system was more inhumane than chattel slavery. Then there were those slave owners who, like Thomas Jefferson, had broken through self-deception to recognize slavery for the sin it was but were too intent upon hanging onto their personal wealth and privilege to abjure it. In their moral cowardice, they traded their slaves' birthright to freedom for a mess of pottage for themselves.

Abolitionists condemned slavery as an offense against charity, the primary virtue taught by Jesus and preached, even if not always practiced, by his followers. Both the Great Commandment to love God and one's fellow human beings, and the Golden Rule, to treat others as one wished to be treated, fell victim to the peculiar institution's erosion of loving empathy for the suffering of others. This absence of fellow-feeling went hand in hand, of course, with the underlying colorphobic assumption that slaves were somehow subhuman creatures who, if they suffered at all under bondage, would do so even more if not protected and cared for by paternalistic white masters. This self-serving condescension on the part of slaveholders presented itself as benevolence, a charade that especially incensed abolitionists.

A final and particularly frightful abolitionist trope in the case against slavery was that the existence of human bondage undermined the strength of the United States by eroding its moral and religious foundations. In genuine prophetic mode, opponents of slavery warned of coming disaster if the nation continued to turn a blind eye to the sin of coerced labor. The warnings generally took two forms. One was that the morally corrupting effects of slavery on slave owners rendered the "master" class lazy, undisciplined, and weak, and therefore easy prey to external enemies. The other was that the slave population, pushed to the limit by its barbaric servitude, inevitably would rise up in revolt on an apocalyptic day of reckoning. God's wrath would descend, and no person who had ever profited however remotely from slavery would be spared. To escape this day of destruction, the nation needed to undergo conversion and moral regeneration, and the first step to that was the abolition of slavery.

In the end, the day of wrath the abolitionists feared was more horrible than they could have imagined: a civil war that claimed six hundred thousand lives. Although the bloodletting culminated in the legal abolition of slavery, it eventually did little, despite the postwar efforts of some abolitionists, to ameliorate the economic condition of blacks or the colorphobia that relegated them to second-class citizenship and third-class opportunities. It would take a second faith-inspired campaign, the civil rights movement of the late 1950s and 1960s, to do something about that.

Nonetheless, the abolitionists are to be admired for their steadfast Christian commitment to human dignity and freedom and their tireless and even sacrificial efforts to pursue justice by preaching and living their faith. As enunciated in the American Anti-Slavery Society's 1833 Declaration of Sentiments, they dedicated themselves heart and soul

> to overthrow the most execrable system of slavery that has ever been witnessed upon earth; to deliver our land from its deadliest curse; to wipe out the foulest stain which rests upon our national escutcheon; and to secure to the colored population of the United States, all the rights and privileges which belong to them as men, and as Americans—come what may to our persons, our interests, or our reputation—whether we live to witness the triumph of Liberty, Justice and Humanity, or perish untimely as martyrs in this great, benevolent, and holy cause.

Theirs was a bright shining moment in both the history of the nation and of faith.

PART ONE

The Colonial Period

The Numerous Afflictions of Joseph

Resolution of
the Germantown Mennonites (1688)

Gerret Henderich, Derick op de Graeff,
Francis Daniell Pastorius, and Abram op de Graeff

*Drafted by four Mennonite converts to Quakerism, the rather mislead-
ingly titled* Resolution *is the earliest extant Christian condemnation of
slavery in the American colonies. Although approved by the Germantown Quaker Meeting in February 1688, it was subsequently tabled
by the Yearly Meeting, presumably because many Quakers in the
Pennsylvania and New Jersey area were slave owners.*

The Resolution's *authors evoke the Golden Rule to condemn
slavery, inviting their Quaker readers to imagine the horror of being
themselves kidnapped and held in bondage. They go on to argue that
owning slaves is both theft and adultery that implicates buyers as well
as sellers of "men-bodies." Surely, they assert, Christians have no "liberty" to do such things. Somewhat startlingly for Quakers, they also
suggest that enslaved blacks have the right to resort to violence in pursuit of their freedom.*

These are the reasons why we are against the traffic of men-body,
as followeth:

Is there any that would be done or handled at this manner?
viz., to be sold or made a slave for all the time of his life? How
fearful and faint-hearted are many at sea, when they see a strange
vessel, being afraid it should be a Turk, and they should be taken,
and sold for slaves into Turkey. Now, what is this better done,

than Turks do? Yea, rather it is worse for them, which say they are
Christians; for we hear that the most part of such negers are
brought hither against their will and consent, and that many of
them are stolen.

Now, though they are black, we cannot conceive there is
more liberty to have them slaves, as it is to have other white
ones. There is a saying that we should do to all men like as we
will be done ourselves; making no difference of what generation,
descent, or color they are. And those who steal or rob men, and
those who buy or purchase them, are they not all alike? Here is
liberty of conscience, which is right and reasonable; here ought
to be likewise liberty of the body, except of evil-doers, which is
another case. But to bring men hither, or to rob and sell them
against their will, we stand against. In Europe there are many oppressed for conscience sake; and here there are those oppressed
which are of a black color. And we, who know that men must not
commit adultery, some do commit adultery in others, separating
wives from their husbands, and giving them to others: and some
sell the children of these poor creatures to other men.

Ah! do consider well this thing, you who do it, if you would
be done at this manner and if it is done according to Christianity!
You surpass Holland and Germany in this thing. This makes an
ill report in all those countries of Europe, where they hear of [it],
that the Quakers do here handle men as they handle there the
cattle. And for that reason some have no mind or inclination to
come hither.

And who shall maintain this your cause, or plead for it?
Truly, we cannot do so, except you shall inform us better hereof,
viz.: that Christians have liberty to practice these things. Pray,
what thing in the world can be done worse towards us, than if
men should rob or steal us away, and sell us for slaves to strange
countries; separating husbands from their wives and children.
Being now this is not done in the manner we would be done at;
therefore, we contradict, and are against this traffic of men-body.
And we who profess that it is not lawful to steal, must, likewise,

avoid to purchase such things as are stolen, but rather help to stop this robbing and stealing, if possible. And such men ought to be delivered out of the hands of the robbers, and set free as in Europe. Then is Pennsylvania to have a good report, instead, it hath now a bad one, for this sake, in other countries; Especially whereas the Europeans are desirous to know in what manner the Quakers do rule in their province; and most of them do look upon us with an envious eye. But if this is done well, what shall we say is done evil?

If once these slaves (which they say are so wicked and stubborn men) should join themselves [to] fight for their freedom, and handle their masters and mistresses, as they did handle them before; will these masters and mistresses take the sword at hand and war against these poor slaves, like, as we are able to believe, some will not refuse to do? Or, have these poor negers not as much right to fight for their freedom, as you have to keep them slaves?

Now consider well this thing, if it is good or bad. And in case you find it to be good to handle these blacks in that manner, we desire and require you hereby lovingly, that you may inform us herein, which at this time never was done, viz., that Christians have such a liberty to do so. To the end we shall be satisfied on this point, and satisfy likewise our good friends and acquaintances in our native country, to whom it is a terror, or fearful thing, that men should be handled so in Pennsylvania.

SOURCE: *The Pennsylvania-German Society Proceedings and Addresses at Allentown, October 14, 1898* (Lancaster, PA: The New Era Printing Company, 1899), 9:197–99.

The Selling of Joseph (1700)

Samuel Sewall

A prominent judge in the Massachusetts Bay Colony, Sewall (1652-1730), one of the magistrates in the Salem witch trials (an involvement he later regretted), was one of Boston's leading slavery opponents. Using the Old Testament story of the selling of Joseph as his inspiration, he argues in the first anti-slavery tract published in New England that "man stealing" is one of the "most atrocious of capital crimes." He takes on and refutes four "Christian" arguments in defense of slavery: blacks are "cursed" descendants of Ham, enslaving Africans exposes them to the gospel, enslaved Africans are lawful captives of war, and the patriarch Abraham had servants. He also points out that slavery morally corrupts owners.

FOR AS MUCH as Liberty is in real value next unto Life:
None ought to part with it themselves,
or deprive others of it, but upon most mature Consideration.

The Numerousness of Slaves at this day in the Province, and the Uneasiness of them under their Slavery, hath put many upon thinking whether the Foundation of it be firmly and well laid; so as to sustain the Vast Weight that is built upon it. It is most certain that all Men, as they are the Sons of *Adam*, are Coheirs; and have equal Right unto Liberty, and all other outward Comforts of Life. GOD *hath given the Earth* (with all its Commodities) *unto the Sons of Adam*, Psalm 115.16. *And hath made of One Blood, all Na-*

tions of Men, for to dwell on all the face of the Earth; and hath deter-mined the Times before appointed, and the bounds of their habitation: That they should seek the Lord. Forasmuch then as we are the Off-spring of GOD etc. Act 17.26, 27, 29. Now although the Title given by the last ADAM, doth infinitely better Men's Estates, re-specting GOD and themselves; and grants them a most beneficial and inviolable Lease under the Broad Seal of Heaven, who were before only Tenants at Will: Yet through the Indulgence of GOD to our First Parents after the Fall, the outward Estate of all and every of the Children, remains the same, as to one another. So that Originally, and Naturally, there is no such thing Slavery.

Joseph was rightfully no more a Slave to his Brethren, than they were to him: and they had no more Authority to *Sell* him, than they had to *Slay* him. And if *they* had nothing to do to Sell him; the *Ishmaelites* bargaining with them, and paying down Twenty pieces of Silver, could not make a Title. Neither could *Potiphar* have any better Interest in him than the *Ish-maelites* had. Gen. 37. 20, 27, 28. For he that shall in this case plead *Alteration of Property*, seems to have forfeited a great part of his own claim to Humanity. There is no proportion between Twenty Pieces of Silver, and LIBERTY. The Commodity itself is the Claimer. If *Arabian* Gold be imported in any quantities, most are afraid to meddle with it, though they might have it at easy rates; lest if it should have been wrongfully taken from the Own-ers, it should kindle a fire to the Consumption of their whole Es-tate. 'Tis pity there should be more Caution used in buying a Horse, or a little lifeless dust; than there is in purchasing Men and Women: Whenas they are the Offspring of GOD, and their Liberty is *Auro pretiosior Omni* [More precious than all gold; cf. Isaiah 13:12].

And seeing GOD hath said, *He that Stealeth a Man and Selleth him, or if he be found in his hand, he shall surely be put to Death.* Exod. 12.16. This Law being of Everlasting Equity, wherein Man Stealing is ranked amongst the most atrocious of Capital Crimes: What louder Cry can there be made of the Celebrated Warning,

Caveat Emptor!

And all things considered, it would conduce more to the Welfare of the Province, to have White Servants for a Term of Years, than to have Slaves for Life. Few can endure to hear of a Negro's being made free; and indeed they can seldom use their freedom well; yet their continual aspiring after their forbidden Liberty, renders them Unwilling Servants. And there is such a disparity in their Conditions, Color & Hair, that they can never embody with us, and grow up into orderly Families, to the Peopling of the Land: but still remain in our Body Politick as a kind of extravasat Blood. As many Negro men as there are among us, so many empty places there are in our Train Bands [local militia units], and the places taken up of Men that might make Husbands for our Daughters. And the Sons and Daughters of *New England* would become more like *Jacob*, and *Rachel*, if this Slavery were thrust quite out of doors. Moreover it is too well known what Temptations Masters are under, to connive at the Fornication of their Slaves; lest they should be obliged to find them Wives, or pay their Fines. It seems to be practically pleaded that they might be Lawless; 'tis thought much of, that the Law should have Satisfaction for their Thefts, and other Immoralities; by which means, *Holiness to the Lord*, is more rarely engraven upon this sort of Servitude. It is likewise most lamentable to think, how in taking Negros out of *Africa*, and Selling of them here, That which GOD has joined together men do boldly rend asunder; Men from their Country, Husbands from their Wives, Parents from their Children. How horrible is the Uncleanness, Mortality, if not Murder, that the Ships are guilty of that bring great Crowds of these miserable Men, and Women. Methinks, when we are bemoaning the barbarous Usage of our Friends and Kinsfolk in *Africa*: it might not be unseasonable to enquire whether we are not culpable in forcing the *Africans* to become Slaves amongst ourselves. And it may be a question whether all the Benefit received by *Negro* Slaves, will balance the Accompt of Cash laid out upon them; and for the Redemption of our own enslaved Friends out of *Africa*. Besides all the Persons and Estates that have perished there.

Obj. 1. *These Blackamores are of the Posterity of Cham [Ham], and therefore are under the Curse of Slavery.* Gen. 9.25, 26, 27.

Answ. Of all Offices, one would not beg this; *viz.* Uncall'd for, to be an Executioner of the Vindictive Wrath of God; the extent and duration of which is to us uncertain. If this ever was a Commission; How do we know but that it is long since out of date? Many have found it to their Cost, that a Prophetical Denunciation of Judgment against a Person or People, would not warrant them to inflict that evil. . . .

Obj. 2. *The Nigers are brought out of a Pagan Country, into places where the Gospel is Preached.*

Answ. Evil must not be done, that good may come of it. The extraordinary and comprehensive Benefit accruing to the Church of God, and to *Joseph* personally, did not rectify his brethren's Sale of him.

Obj. 3. *The Africans have Wars with one another: our Ships bring lawful Captives taken in those Wars.*

Answ. For ought is known, their Wars are much such as were between *Jacob's* Sons and their Brother *Joseph*. If they be between Town and Town; Provincial, or National: Every War is upon one side Unjust. An Unlawful War can't make lawful Captives. And by Receiving, we are in danger to promote, and partake in their Barbarous Cruelties. I am sure, if some Gentlemen should go down to the *Brewsters* to take the Air, and Fish: And a stronger party from *Hull* should Surprise them, and Sell them for Slaves to a Ship outward bound: they would think themselves unjustly dealt with; both by Sellers and Buyers. And yet 'tis to be feared, we have no other kind of Title to our *Nigers*. *Therefore all things whatsoever ye would that men should do to you, do ye even so to them: for this is the Law and the Prophets.* Matt. 7. 12.

Obj. 4. Abraham *had servants bought with his Money, and born in his House.*

Answ. Until the Circumstances of *Abraham's* purchase be recorded, no Argument can be drawn from it. In the meantime, Charity obliges us to conclude, that He knew it was lawful and good.

It is Observable that the *Israelites* were strictly forbidden the buying, or selling one another for Slaves. Levit. 25. 39, 46. Jer. 34. 8—22 ... GOD expects that Christians should be of a more Ingenuous and benign frame of spirit. Christians should carry it to all the World, as the *Israelites* were to carry it towards another. And for men obstinately to persist in holding their Neighbors and Brethren under the Rigor of perpetual Bondage, seems to be no proper way of gaining Assurance that God has given them Spiritual Freedom. Our Blessed Savior has altered the Measures of the Ancient Love-Song, and set it to a most Excellent New Tune, which all ought to be ambitious of Learning. Matt. 5. 43, 44. John 13. 34.

These *Ethiopians*, as black as they are; seeing they are the Sons and Daughters of the First *Adam*, the Brethren and Sister of the Last ADAM, and the Offspring of GOD; They ought to be treated with a Respect agreeable.

SOURCE: Samuel Sewall, *The Selling of Joseph: A Memorial* (Boston: Bartholomew Green and John Allen, Printers, 1700).

All Slave-Keepers
that Keep the Innocent in Bondage,
Apostates (1737)

Benjamin Lay

Quaker Benjamin Lay (1682–1759) saw firsthand the cruelty of slavery when he migrated from England to Barbados, an island where captured Africans drudged on sugar cane plantations. After leaving the Caribbean for Philadelphia, he became a tireless critic of human bondage, exhorting fellow Quakers to repent and free their slaves. Lay often punctuated his words with dramatic acts. Right after the publication of All Slave-Keepers, *he shocked Philadelphia Quakers during a sermon against slavery by plunging a sword into a bible to shoot a spout of "blood"—pokeberry juice hidden away in a bladder—on his audience. His message, that slave owners had blood on their hands, came through loud and clear.*

In this selection from All Slave-Keepers, *Lay pleads for moral consistency in his fellow Quakers. They cannot in good faith denounce war if they participate in or even only tolerate the violence of slavery. They must remember that they are called to be examples of rectitude to others, and keeping slaves ill accords with that obligation. Finally, drawing on his observance of the brutality of slavery during his years in Barbados, he condemns the drudgery of life as a slave as well as the arrogance in the life of a master.*

No greater nor no better Law, say I, than to love God above all, and all our Fellow-Creatures as ourselves; these two contain Law,

Prophets and Gospel, do to all as we would be done by. No greater Sin Hell can invent, than to profane and blaspheme the pure and Holy Truth, which is God all in all, and remove God's Creatures made after his own Image, from all the Comforts of Life, and their Country and procure for them, and bring them into all the miseries that Dragons, Serpents, Devils, and Hypocrites, can procure and think of; these things are carried on by Christians, so called, and Ministers too, in the very greatest appearance of Demurity [sic] and Sanctity in the whole World that ever I read or heard of; God which is the Truth, saith we shall not eat the cursed Fruit; our Ministers say we may eat, and lawfully too; which shall we believe?

We pretend not to love fighting with carnal Weapons, nor to carry Swords by our sides, but carry a worse thing in the Heart, as will, I believe appear by and by; what, I pray and beseech you, dear Friends, by the tender Mercies of our God, to consider, can be greater Hypocrisy, and plainer contradiction, than for us as a People, to refuse to bear Arms, or to pay them that do, and yet purchase the Plunder, the Captives, for Slaves at a very great Price, thereby justifying their selling of them, and the War, by which they were or are obtained; nor doth this satisfy, but their Children also are kept in Slavery, *ad infinitum;* is not this plainly and substantially trampling the most Blessed and Glorious Testimony that ever was or ever will be in the World, under our Feet, and committing of Iniquity with, both Hands earnestly? Is this the way to convince the poor Slaves, or our Children, or Neighbors, or the World? Is it not the way rather to encourage and strengthen them in their Infidelity, and Atheism, and their Hellish Practice of Fighting, Murdering, killing and Robbing one another, to the end of the World?

My dear friends, I beg, I would entreat, in all Humility, with all earnestness of mind, on the bended Knees of my Body and Soul; willingly and with all readiness, sincerely, if that would do, that you would turn to the Lord, the Blessed Truth, in your Hearts, for Direction, for Counsel and Advice; that you may quit your selves like Men, honorably, of this so Hellish a Practice. Especially, you that have the Word of Reconciliation to preach to the Children of Men; and if you have any true tenderness of the Love of God in you, as I right well know, blessed be the Name of the Lord, all true Ministers have, you my dear Friends, consider weightily of these important concerns, and quit yourselves of yourselves and Slaves; for a good example in you might do a great deal of good, as a bad one will do, and has done a very great deal of mischief to the Truth; for the Eyes of the People are upon you, some for good, and some for Evil.

And my Friends, you that have Slaves, and do minister to others in our Meetings, consider I entreat and beseech you concerning this thing in particular. What Burdens and Afflictions, Bondage, and sore Captivity you bring upon your dear and tender Friends, and keep them in, which cannot touch with this vile and Hellish Practice, but are constrained to bear Testimony against it, as one of the greatest Sins in the World, all things considered. And against you too in some sort, as being in the practice yourselves, of that which is directly opposite to your own Pretensions, and a very great stumbling Block in the way of honest, godly Inquirers, which want Peace to their Souls.

What a great Strait these tender hearted mourning Souls must needs be in, think ye, betwixt Love and Duty; they love you dearly for the Truth's sake, and yet think it their Duty absolutely in the Fear and Love of God, to testify against the Sin, and you for continuing in it.

Dear Friends, what Peace can you have, in thus afflicting your Fellow Members; even the same Testimony they have with you in Meetings, where is the Blessed Unity and Fellowship, you have been preaching so many Years, as being sensible of one another's exercises, Bearers of one another's Burdens, having a deep sense and feeling of others' infirmities, or afflictions, or troubles?...

For Custom in Sin, hides, covers, as it were takes away the Guilt of Sin. Long Custom, the Conveniency of Slaves working for us, waiting and tending continually on us, beside the Washing, cleaning, scouring, cooking very nicely fine and curious, sewing, knitting, darning, almost ever at hand and Command; and in other Places milking, churning, Cheese-making, and all the Drudgery in Dairy and Kitchen, within doors and without. And the proud, dainty, lazy Daughters sit with their Hands before 'em, like some of the worst idle Sort of Gentlewomen, and if they want a Trifle, rather than rise from their Seats, call the poor Slave from her Drudgery to come and wait upon them. These Things have been the utter Ruin of more than a few; and yet encouraged by their own Parents, for whom my Spirit is grieved, some of which were and are Preachers in great Repute as well as others.

Now, dear Friends, behold a Mystery! These Ministers that be Slave-keepers, and are in such very great Repute, such eminent Preachers, given to Hospitality, charitable to the Poor, loving to their Neighbors, just in their Dealings, temperate in their Lives, visiting of the Sick, sympathizing with the Afflicted in Body or Mind, very religious seemingly, and extraordinary [sic] devout and demure, and in short strictly exact in all their Decorums, except Slave-keeping, these, these be the Men, and the Women too, for the Devil's purpose, and are the choicest Treasure the Devil can or has to bring out of his Lazaretto, to establish Slave-keeping. By these Satan works wonders many ways. These are the very Men, or People of both Sexes, that come the nearest the Scribes & Pharisees of any People in the whole World, if not sincere: For the Scribes were exact and demure seemingly in their Appearance before Men, according to Christ's Account of them, and yet the worst Enemies the dear Lamb had, or that the Devil could procure for or against him. And I do surely believe that one such as these, now in this our Day, in this very Country, does more Service for the Devil, and Hurt in the Church, in Slave-keeping, than twenty Publicans and Harlots. For by their extraordinary Conduct, in Hypocrisy, smooth and plausible appearance, they draw into the

Snare almost insensibly, and so beguile unstable Souls before they are aware, which is sorrowful to consider as well as write, their Example being much more powerful than others.

And Friends, what I touched at a little before, concerning the delicate Damsels, or fine idle Dames, it may be pretty much like it with the young Men, and may be the old ones, that have their Negroes to Plow, sow, thresh, winnow, split Rails, cut Wood, clear Land, make Ditches and Fences, fodder Cattle, run and fetch up the Horses, or fine curious pacing Mares, for young Madam and Sir to ride about on, impudently and proudly gossiping from House to House stuffing their lazy ungodly Bellies. Then old Sir Master calls, *Negro, fetch my best Gelding quickly, for me to ride to Meeting, to preach the Gospel of glad Tidings to all Men, and Liberty to the Captives, and opening the Prison-Doors to them that are bound; but I'll keep thee in Bondage nevertheless, help thy self if thee can. I charge thee to work very hard when I am gone, and before be very ready to wait on me & my Children when we come home, if they come with me, or else wait till they do come, and then take their Horses, and look well after them; and then make haste in, all of ye, and be ready to wait upon us, and keep good Fires above stairs or below, and mind your Business well, or I'll take a Course with you; don't think that I'll give 70 or 80 pounds apiece for you, for nothing but to lie lazing about like Gentlemen, doing nothing you shall work now you are young, for when you are very old, you will not do much, I suppose, and then you must be maintained, you and your Wives and Children and Children's Children; and if you don't behave yourselves well, you'll be but badly provided for, I believe, when you are past your Labor, whatever you are now.*

Dear friends, these Things are true in Fact, and have been the Ruin of many, Body and Soul, and will be of more I greatly fear; beside and above all, the soul Stain it brings upon the pure, blessed, unchangeable TRUTH.

And my dear, my very dear Friends, I must say, I must say, and it is the Experience and certain Knowledge of my own Soul, that except People will be willing to come to a Separation, a Separation, a Separation,

from	this	Thing,
to wit,	Negro	Practice,

they never can nor will see the Evil of it, as it really is in itself.

I say my own Experience when I lived in Barbados about 18 years ago, where we had much Business in Trading, and the poor Blacks would come to our Shop and Store, hunger-starved, almost ready to perish with Hunger and Sickness, great Numbers of them would come to trade with us, for they seemed to love and admire us, we being pretty much alike in Stature and other ways; and my dear Wife would often be giving them something for the Mouth, which was very engaging you that read this may be sure, in their deplorable Condition. Oh! My Soul mourns in contemplating their miserable, forlorn, wretched State and Condition that mine Eyes beheld them in then, and it is the same now, and will remain except the great almighty Being, either immediately or instrumentally shall be pleased to put a Stop to it; for they are yearly by Shiploads poured in upon, and received by the People, many Thousands in one Year, Year after Year, as is thought, up and down America, besides what vast Numbers are increased by Generation daily. O Lord God Almighty, where will this Practice lead us that are called thy People, Dearest God, and make so great a Profession of being led and guided by thy eternal Spirit, which is the glorious Truth unchangeable and precious, and without End. But I trust, dearest One, thou wilt be pleased to stop and end this Practice, that is more like hell than Heaven, to be sure.

SOURCE: Benjamin Lay, *All Slave-Keepers that keep the innocent in bondage, apostates pretending to lay claim to the pure & holy Christian religion; of what congregation so ever but especially in their ministers* (Philadelphia: Printed for the Author, 1737), 10–13, 28–33.

Considerations on the Keeping of Negroes
(1754)

John Woolman

Gentle John Woolman (1720–1772), an itinerant Quaker preacher so opposed to human bondage that he insisted on paying slaves who served him when he visited the homes of slave owners, acknowledges in his Considerations *that some masters might be found who treat their slaves kindly. But despite that, the institution violates the Christian principle of brotherhood and sisterhood, a principle that ought to encourage empathy. Enslaving others arises from and exacerbates a "darkness in the understanding" that inhibits empathy, and is thus contrary to the true interests of both slave and slave owner.*

As many times there are different motives to the same action; and one does that from a generous heart, which another does for selfish ends; the like may be said in this case.

There are various circumstances among those that keep negroes, and different ways by which they fall under their care; and I doubt not, there are many well-disposed persons amongst them who desire rather to manage wisely and justly in this difficult matter, than to make gain of it.

But the general disadvantage which these poor negroes lie under in an enlightened Christian country, having often filled me with real sadness, I now think it my duty, through Divine aid, to offer some thoughts thereon to the consideration of others.

When we remember that all nations are of one blood, (Gen. iii. 20,) that in this world we are but sojourners, that we

17

are subject to the like afflictions and infirmities of body, the like disorders and frailties in mind, the like temptations, the same death, and the same judgment, and that the all-wise Being is Judge and Lord over us all, it seems to raise an idea of general brotherhood, and a disposition easy to be touched with a feeling of each other's afflictions: but when we forget those things, and look chiefly at our outward circumstances, in this and some ages past, constantly retaining in our minds the distinction between us and them, with respect to our knowledge and improvement in things Divine, natural and artificial, our breasts being apt to be filled with fond notions of superiority, there is danger of erring in our conduct toward them....

To consider mankind otherwise than brethren, to think favors are peculiar to one nation, and to exclude others, plainly supposes a darkness in the understanding: for as God's love is universal, so where the mind is sufficiently influenced by it, it begets a likeness of itself, and the heart is enlarged towards all men. Again, to conclude a people forward, perverse, and worse by nature than others, who ungratefully receive favors, and apply them to bad ends, will excite a behavior toward them unbecoming the excellence of true religion....

When self-love presides in our minds, our opinions are biased in our own favor; and in this condition, being concerned with a people so situated that they have no voice to plead their own cause, there is danger of using ourselves to an undisturbed partiality, until, by long custom, the mind becomes reconciled with it, and the judgment itself infected.

To apply humbly to God for wisdom, that we may thereby be enabled to see things as they are, and as they ought to be, is very needful. Hereby the hidden things of darkness may be brought to light, and the judgment made clear: we shall then consider mankind as brethren. Though different degrees and a variety of qualifications and abilities, one dependent on another, be admitted, yet high thoughts will be laid aside, and all men treated as becometh the sons of one father, agreeably to the doctrine of

Christ Jesus. "He hath laid down the best criterion, by which mankind ought to judge of their own conduct, and others judge for them of theirs, one towards another, viz. 'Whatsoever ye would that men should do unto you, do ye even so to them.' I take it, that all men by nature are equally entitled to the equity of this rule, and under the indispensable obligations of it. One man ought not to look upon another man or society of men as so far beneath him that he should not put himself in their place, in all his actions towards them, and bring all to this test, viz. How should I approve of this conduct, were I in their circumstance, and they in mine?"*

This doctrine being of a moral unchangeable nature, hath been likewise inculcated in the former dispensation; "If a stranger sojourn with thee in your land, ye shall not vex him; but the stranger that dwelleth with you shall be as one born amongst you, and thou shalt love him as thyself." Had these people [slaves] come voluntarily and dwelt amongst us, to call them strangers would be proper; and their being brought by force, with regret and a languishing mind, may well raise compassion in a heart rightly disposed: but there is nothing in such treatment which, upon a wise and judicious consideration, will in any way lessen their right to be treated as strangers. If the treatment which many of them meet with be rightly examined, and compared with those precepts, "Thou shalt not vex him nor oppress him; he shall be as one born amongst you, and thou shalt love him as thyself," there will appear an important difference between them....

[The Most High's] love is not confined, but extends to the stranger; and to excite their compassion, reminds them of times past, "Ye were strangers in the land of Egypt." Again, "Thou shalt not oppress a stranger, for ye know the heart of a stranger, seeing ye

---

*Alexander Arscott, *Some Considerations Relating to the Present State of the Christian Religion* (1731), III, fol. 107. Arscott's book was extremely popular in Woolman's lifetime. By 1779, thirty editions of it had been printed.

were strangers in the land of Egypt" [Exodus 23:9]. If we call to mind our beginning, some of us may find a time, wherein our fathers were under afflictions, reproaches, and manifold sufferings....

If we, by the operation of the Spirit of Christ, become heirs with him in the kingdom of his Father, and are redeemed from the alluring counterfeit joys of this World, and the joy of Christ remain in us; to suppose that one in this happy condition can, for the sake of earthly riches, not only deprive his fellow-creatures of the sweetness of freedom, which, rightly used, is one of the greatest temporal blessings, but therewith neglect using proper means for their acquaintance with the Holy Scriptures, and the advantage of true religion, seems at least a contradiction to reason.

Whoever rightly advocates the cause of some, thereby promotes the good of all. The state of mankind was harmonious in the beginning, and though sin hath introduced discord, yet through the wonderful love of God in Christ Jesus our Lord, the way is open for our redemption, and means appointed to restore us to primitive harmony. That if one suffer by the unfaithfulness of another, the mind, the most noble part of him that occasions the discord, is thereby alienated from its true and real happiness.

Our duty and interest are inseparably united, and when we neglect or misuse our talents, we necessarily depart from the heavenly fellowship, and are in the way to the greatest of evils. Therefore to examine and prove ourselves, to find what harmony the power presiding in us bears with the Divine nature, is a duty not more incumbent and necessary, than it would be beneficial.

SOURCE: John Woolman, *Considerations on the Keeping of Negroes, recommended to the Professors of Christianity of Every Denomination* (Philadelphia: Tract Association of Friends, [n.d.]), 3–5, 6–7, 9–11.

Letter to the Rev. Samson Occom (1774)

Phyllis Wheatley

A West African who was stolen from her homeland when she was a young child and sold into slavery in Boston, Wheatley (c. 1753–1784) was the first black poet published in North America. Freed at the age of twenty following the publication of a book of poems, she subsequently married. But her husband was sent to debtor's prison and Wheatley, forced to do physical labor to make ends meet, died before a second volume of poetry could be published.

Samson Occom was a member of the Mohegan nation who had converted to Christianity during the Great Awakening and was subsequently ordained a Presbyterian minister. Wheatley's letter to him is an affirmation of his public criticism of Christian clergy who owned slaves. Regardless of birthplace or culture, she writes, all humans have a fundamental love of freedom implanted in them by the Creator that is "impatient of Oppression and pants for Deliverance."

Rev'd and honor'd Sir,

I have this Day received your obliging kind Epistle, and am greatly satisfied with your Reasons respecting the Negroes, and think highly reasonable what you offer in Vindication of their natural Rights: Those that invade them cannot be insensible that the divine Light is chasing away the thick Darkness which broods over the Land of Africa; and the Chaos which has reign'd so long, is converting into beautiful Order, and reveals more and more clearly, the glorious Dispensation of civil and religious Liberty, which are so inseparably Limited, that there is little or no Enjoyment of one Without the other: Otherwise, perhaps, the Israelites had been less solicitous for their Freedom from Egyptian slavery; I do not say they would have been contented without it, by no means, for in every human Breast, God has implanted a Principle, which we call Love of Freedom; it is impatient of Oppression, and pants for Deliverance; and by the Leave of our modern Egyptians I will assert, that the same Principle lives in us. God grant Deliverance in his own Way and Time, and get him honor upon all those whose Avarice impels them to countenance and help forward vile Calamities of their fellow Creatures. This I desire not for their Hurt, but to convince them of the strange Absurdity of their Conduct whose Words and Actions are so diametrically, opposite. How well the Cry for Liberty, and the reverse Disposition for the exercise of oppressive Power over others agree—I humbly think it does not require the Penetration of a Philosopher to determine.

SOURCE: Letter to *The Connecticut Gazette* (March 1774).

PART TWO

THE EARLY REPUBLIC

Terrible in Crime and Magnitude

African Distress (1788)

Theodore Dwight

A grandson of theologian Jonathan Edwards, Theodore Dwight (1764–1846) was a lawyer by profession and a poet by avocation. One of New Haven, Connecticut's, staunchest opponents of slavery, he wrote these verses, as he says in his prose prologue, after hearing of Guinean families being ripped apart by slavers. In having the despairing mother and sister address themselves to the "God of Christians," Dwight's implied indictment of his fellow religionists who defend slave trade is especially poignant. He forces them to ask themselves if their acquiescence to "the barbarous traffic of human flesh" means that the God they worship is, in fact, a cruel and fierce idol.

The distress which the inhabitants of Guinea experience at the loss of their children, which are stolen from them by the persons employed in the barbarous traffic of human flesh, is, perhaps, more thoroughly felt than described. But, as it is a subject to which every person has not attended, the Author of the following lines hopes that, possibly, he may excite some attention, (while he obtains indulgence) to an attempt to represent the anguish of a mother, whose son and daughter were taken from her by a Ship's Crew, belonging to a Country where the GOD of Justice and Mercy is owned and worshipped.

"HELP! oh, help! thou God of Christians!
    Save a mother from despair!
Cruel white men steal my children!
    God of Christians, hear my prayer!

"From my arms by force they're rended,
    Sailors drag them to the sea;
Yonder ship, at anchor riding,
    Swift will carry them away.

"There my son lies, stripp'd, and bleeding;
    Fast, with thongs, his hands are bound.
See, the tyrants, how they scourge him!
    See his sides a reeking wound

"See his little sister by him;
    Quaking, trembling, how she lies!
Drops of blood her face besprinkle;
    Tears of anguish fill her eyes.

"Now they tear her brother from her;
    Down, below the deck, he's thrown;
Stiff with beating, through fear silent,
    Save a single, death-like, groan."

Hear the little creature begging!—
    "Take me, white men, for your own!
Spare, oh, spare my darling brother!
    He's my mother's only son.

"See, upon the shore she's raving:
    Down she falls upon the sands:
Now, she tears her flesh with madness;
    Now, she prays with lifted hands.

"I am young, and strong, and hardy;
    He's a sick, and feeble boy;
Take me, whip me, chain me, starve me,
    All my life I'll toil with joy.

"Christians! who's the God you worship?
    Is he cruel, fierce, or good?
Does he take delight in mercy?
    Or in spilling human blood?

"Ah, my poor distracted mother!
    Hear her scream upon the shore."—
Down the savage captain struck her,
    Lifeless on the vessel's floor.

Up his sails he quickly hoisted,
    To the ocean bent his way;
Headlong plunged the raving mother,
    From a high rock, in the sea.

SOURCE: E. H. Smith, ed., *American Poems, Selected and Original* (Litchfield, CT: Collier and Buel, 1793), 1: 217–19.

APPEAL TO THE COLORED CITIZENS
OF THE WORLD (1829)

DAVID WALKER

A free black and used clothing dealer in Boston, David Walker (1796–1830) scandalized the white world when his Appeal *appeared a year before his death. In it, he warned of an uprising of both enslaved and free blacks if the injustices inflicted upon them continued. His book was widely and surreptitiously distributed in southern seaports by northern black sailors, and was quickly outlawed by several slave-state legislatures. Some southern states offered a bounty for Walker's capture or assassination.*

In this selection from the book's third edition, Walker blasts the open and unabashed oppression of blacks practiced by Christians who, in writing oppressive laws regulating the lives of slaves, no longer even bother to hide their iniquities "under a garb of humanity and religion." As an illustration of white Christians' perfidy, he refers to an "act of cruelty" inflicted on a black man by Boston's Park Street Church. In 1830, Frederick Brinsley, who held legal ownership to a pew in the otherwise all-white church, was blocked by church elders from occupying it. They threatened him with arrest if he persisted in asserting his right to the pew, eventually forcing him to relinquish it and withdraw from the church.

Our dear Redeemer said, "Therefore, whatsoever ye have spoken in darkness, shall be heard in the light; and that which ye have spoken in the ear in closets, shall be proclaimed upon the house tops" [Luke 12:3].

How obviously this declaration of our Lord has been shown among the Americans of the United States. They have hitherto passed among some nations, who do not know anything about their internal concerns, for the most enlightened, humane, charitable, and merciful people upon earth, when at the same time they treat us, (the colored people) secretly more cruel and unmerciful than any other nation upon earth.

It is a fact, that in our Southern and Western States, there are millions who hold us in chains or in slavery, whose greatest object and glory, is centered in keeping us sunk in the most profound ignorance and stupidity, to make us work without remunerations for our services. Many of whom if they catch a colored person, whom they hold in unjust ignorance, slavery and degradation, to them and their children, with a book in his hand, will beat him nearly to death. I heard a wretch in the state of North Carolina said, that if any man would teach a black person whom he held in slavery, to spell, read or write, he would prosecute him to the very extent of the law. Said the ignorant wretch, "a Nigar, ought not to have any more sense than enough to work for his master." May I not ask to fatten the wretch and his family?

These and similar cruelties these *Christians* have been for hundreds of years inflicting on our fathers and us in the dark, God has however, very recently published some of their secret crimes on the house top, that the world may gaze on their Christianity and see of what kind it is composed.

Georgia for instance, God has completely shown to the world, the *Christianity* among its white *inhabitants*. A law has recently passed the Legislature of this *republican* State (Georgia) prohibiting all free or slave persons of color, from learning to read or write; another law has passed the *republican* House of Delegates, (but not the Senate) in Virginia, to prohibit all persons of color, (free and slave) from learning to read or write, and even to hinder them from meeting together in order to worship our Maker!!!!!!

Now I solemnly appeal, to the most skillful historians in the world, and all those who are mostly acquainted with the histories of the Antediluvians and of Sodom and Gomorrah, to show me a parallel of barbarity. *Christians!! Christians!!!* I dare you to show me a parallel of cruelties in the annals of Heathens or of Devils, with those of Ohio, Virginia and of Georgia—know the world that these things were before done in the dark, or in a corner under a garb of humanity and religion. God has however, taken off the fig-leaf covering, and made them expose themselves on the house top. I tell you that God works in many ways his wonders to perform, he will unless they repent, make them expose themselves enough more yet to the world.

See the acts of the *Christians* in FLORIDA, SOUTH CAROLINA, and KENTUCKY—was it not for the reputation of the house of my Lord and Master, I would mention here, an act of cruelty inflicted a few days since on a black man, by the white *Christians* in the PARK STREET CHURCH, in this (CITY) which is almost enough to make Demons themselves quake and tremble in their FIREY HABITATIONS.

Oh! my Lord how refined in iniquity the whites have got to be in consequence of our blood—what kind!! Oh! what kind!!! of Christianity can be found this day in all the earth!!!!!!

I write without the fear of man, I am writing for my God, and fear none but himself; they may put me to death if they choose— (I fear and esteem a good man however, let him be black or white.) I forbear to comment on the cruelties inflicted on this Black Man by the Whites, in the Park Street MEETING HOUSE, I will leave it in the dark!!!!! But I declare that the atrocity is really to Heaven daring and infernal, that I must say that God has commenced a course of exposition among the Americans, and the glorious and heavenly work will continue to progress until they learn to do justice.

SOURCE: *Walker's Appeal, in Four Articles; together with a preamble, to the Coloured Citizens of the world, but in particular, and ever expressly, to those of the United States of America.* 3rd edition. (Boston: privately printed, 1830), 58–61.

Excommunicate Slaveholders (1830)

Thomas Doan

Thomas Doan (1781–1851) was a founding member and first clerk of a branch of the Tennessee Manumission Society organized in Jefferson County on February 25, 1815. One of the society's requirements was that members prominently display a sign in the "most conspicuous" place of their homes that read: "Freedom is the natural right of all men, I therefore acknowledge myself a member of the Tennessee Society for promoting the manumission of slaves."

The Jefferson branch appears to have lasted until the early 1830s. On May 1, 1830, Doan addressed its members, urging them to reignite the anti-slavery zeal that had led to the organization's founding in the first place. He also urged his fellow Christians to consider excommunicating slaveholding Christians until they liberated their slaves.

Fellow helpers in pleading the cause of the poor and the needy: were it not for the too general apathy which prevails over a large number of the professed advocates for African freedom, I should despair of bring forward a single idea that was new, or of casting the least glimmer of undiscovered light upon the subject—so nearly has it been exhausted by the numerous speakers and writers that have from time to time treated upon it. But on account of the general apathy, of which I have been speaking, I have made the venture....

In addressing you at this time, I must beg of such of you, if such there be, that are almost "twice dead and plucked up by the

31

roots" [Jude 1:12], to awake from your sleep of stupefaction, and arise from your graves of insensibility, and exercise a little more energy in attending your meetings for promoting the object of the institution of which you are members....

Let me now call your attention back to the first formation of your human institution, and ask you then what was the appearance, and what the prospect? A few "earthen pitchers and their lamps" [Judges 7:16], assaying to contend with almost a whole nation of inveterate slaveholders! The prospect, to mortal eyes, was gloomy indeed; and the appearance not less contemptible to the surrounding hosts of slaveholders than the stripling David was to the mail-coated Goliath of Gath.

But let us mark the revolving rounds of only fourteen years, and test the changes which have taken place within that period. The principle which you then advocated might be compared to the "little cloud of a size of a man's hand" [1 Kings 18:44]; or perhaps more fitly to the "little leaven, hid in the meal" [Matthew 13:33]; but what now is its appearance? Why, that same "little leaven"—that same principle of freedom which you contended for—has exerted its influence, not only over this large continent, but over Spanish America also, and has even found its way into the British Parliament; nor do I believe that its salutary effects will cease, till the "whole lump is leavened" and the curse of slavery eradicated from the civilized world.

Thousands, fellow helpers, who were the avowed enemies of African emancipation fourteen short years ago, have been convinced, and are now among the warmest advocates for freedom. Your numbers, as friends to the rights of man, have increased beyond your most sanguine expectations. In the infancy of your institution, your enemies viewed you with contempt—they neither loved nor feared you nor your efforts; but many, who then considered you as almost beneath their notice, to them you now have a formidable appearance, and they dread the effects of your exertions and existence....

This is the most delicate part of my general subject, and I would willingly have left it unnoticed, did I not believe that duty urged me to the contrary. Shall I thus publicly venture to tell my fears, and not be in danger of being called an infidel? To avoid this, let me first state without hypocrisy that I am a believer in the Christian religion, and some sort of an unworthy professor of it. Having thus premised, I proceed: I fear, fellow helpers, that a majority, perhaps, of the Christian professing societies in our country, are amongst the greatest props, supporters, and upholders of the system of slavery, of any other class of citizens whatever. The most, if not all of them, acknowledge slavery to be wrong, and pronounce it to be both a national sin and a moral evil; and yet keep slaveholders in church communion, and some of them have slaveholding preachers, and authorize them to be instructors of others in the mysteries of Christianity!

There is something a little mysterious in this: pronounce a slaveholder to be a moral sinner, and then authorize the same moral sinner to preach the pure gospel of the Redeemer! Pronounce the slaveholding lay member to be a moral sinner, and then unite with him in full Christian fellowship, in performing the most sacred acts of Christian devotion, by communing together at the eucharist board and in the full fellowship-denoting love feast; of the flesh-purifying operation of washing feet! There appears to me to be either a great inconsistency in these things, or a most intolerable daubing with untampered mortar.

How do you feel, fellow manumissionists, when you join with slaveholders in any or all of the above described emblems of Christian fellowship? Or when you sit under the droppings of the sanctuary of a slaveholding preacher? Do you feel no revoltings of mind upon such occasions? Reflect, if you please, and think upon it. I am fully persuaded, that if all the Christian churches in America excommunicate every slaveholding member who should refuse to manumit his or her slaves, and finally exclude all such from becoming members in future, that it would do more in breaking every yoke, undoing the heavy burdens, and letting the oppressed go free, than any means which ever have been, or can be, used against it.

SOURCE: *Genius of Universal Emancipation* (Nov. 1830), 3rd Series: Vol. 1, #8.

Three Essays (1830s)

Elizabeth Margaret Chandler

There were few American abolitionists as talented as Quaker Elizabeth Margaret Chandler (1807–1834). Born in Pennsylvania but having migrated to Michigan in 1830, at that time a rough frontier, she contributed a regular column, the "Ladies Repository," to Benjamin Lundy's abolitionist newspaper The Genius of Universal Emancipation. *In her column she urged women to recognize the strength and energy they brought to the abolitionist cause, notwithstanding their reputation as the "weaker sex." Her premature death was a great loss to the movement. Lundy published two posthumous volumes of her poetry and essays.*

In the three selections from her "Ladies Repository" here, Chandler chides women for the fatalistic attitude that nothing can be done by them to end human bondage and reminds them that their Christian duty is to persevere for charity's sake, not worrying about the outcome of their endeavors.

INDIFFERENCE

We believe it is generally acknowledged that there is more danger to be apprehended to any cause, from the lukewarmness of its pretended friends, than from the bitterest hostility of its professed enemies. The attacks of the one will always rouse up opponents to repel them. The lethargy of the other palsies even the hand of zeal, and infects with a benumbing influence the energies of the warmest hearted. It is this lifelessness, this apathy, that is the more dangerous enemy to the cause of Emancipation. We have been frequently astonished at the perfect indifference manifested when this subject is adverted to, even by those whom we might suppose would be most easily interested, and among some who openly profess to reprobate the system of slavery. You may speak of the wrongs and sufferings of our colored population; you may tell them of all the evils attendant upon slavery; you may recount, if they will listen to you so long, a harrowing tale of human misery, till your own cheek burns, and heart swells at the recital, and when you have concluded, they will turn coldly away, and answer, "All this may be very true—but why do you tell it to us? the fault is not ours, nor the remedy in our power; it is useless, therefore, to distress ourselves with the thought of wretchedness which we cannot relieve."

Yet they will almost always conclude with acknowledging that the system of slavery is both criminal and disgraceful, and with a wish that it was abolished altogether—while at the same time, to judge from their conduct, they seem perfectly determined not to raise so much as a little finger in aid of that object. "And what more can we do," such persons may perhaps exclaim, "than to give our best wishes to the cause of emancipation?" You can do a great deal more—you can give it your active exertions—and you must do so, if you would ever behold the day when the cry of the oppressed shall be heard no more "within our borders." You should form yourselves into societies for the opposition of slavery. Your interest will, by that means, be kept awake, you will have better opportunities both of acquiring and diffusing information upon the subject, and your aid, altogether, will be more effective.

Nor should you imagine you have completed your duty by declaring yourselves the enemies of oppression—you should endeavor to prevail upon your friends to do likewise. The subject is one of the utmost importance, both to the moral and political interests of our country, and should occupy your thoughts, and be made the theme of your conversation, not only in your stated meetings for its discussion, but while you are engaged in your daily occupations, or when you have gathered into a friendly circle around the evening hearth.

We do not expect the influence of women to have any immediate or perceptible effect upon the councils of the Senatehouse—but let their efforts be steadily directed to arousing the public mind to the importance of this subject, and keeping awake that attention by every means in their power, and we have no doubt but they will be speedily and beneficially felt. It is useless to talk of the difficulties of the case, of the danger of intermeddling with a subject which even men approach with timidity, and of the total impossibility of our effecting any change in the course of circumstances. We do not see the least impossibility in the matter, and we deny that there is any. But we do know that it is impossible to remove from the bosom of our country a crime that should weigh her plumed head in shame to the very dust, by sitting passively down, and wishing it were otherwise. That there may be difficulties in the case, we admit, but it would be absurd to suppose that it is entirely without remedy. Let the general attention be but thoroughly excited, let men be forced into the necessity of acting, and efficient remedial measures will soon be devised and adopted: and so we may yet see the folds of our "starspangled banner" floating unsullied on the free air, and the dark sin, which hath so long polluted our country, atoned for and forgiven.

OUR DUTIES

"It will do no good"—is an answer we have received so often, when endeavoring to awaken our friends to the subject of emancipation, that we are positively weary of hearing it repeated, and almost out of patience—just as if the success or failure of our endeavors could in the least affect the question of right or wrong! Is the performance of duties to God and our fellow-creatures the less emphatically urged upon us, because we choose to imagine it will have no effect on the mass of human crime and misery? Nay, is there not even guilt in such reasoning? Because we think that other people will do wrong in spite of our efforts to prevent them, should we join in upholding them in their iniquity, and participate with them in the enjoyment of the fruits of it? And in such a case we need scarcely demand, which would be most deeply criminal—those who thoughtlessly and blindly press forward on a career of guilt, or those, who, fully awake to its sinfulness, persist in lending their support?

That the system of slavery, as existing among us in the very bosom of these free States, is a dark outrage upon justice and humanity, we presume there are few among our own sex hardy enough to dispute. If there be any such, they must daringly maintain a false argument in the very face of conscience, or have been, strangely blinded by a long series of years of prejudice.

But what signifies our combating an evil that we can never subdue? What signifies a conscience void of offence in the sight of the everlasting One? What signifies the calm retrospective reflection of the twilight hour, broken in upon by no secret consciousness of blood-guiltiness? It is only for you to act, and to leave to Him—the Omnipotent—the judgment and direction of your usefulness. Because you, in the short-sightedness of mortality, behold no way for the redemption out of their bonds, of an oppressed people, is His power limited, "His hand shortened, that it cannot save?" And have we not good grounds for believing, that on the offering, however humble, of a sincere and contrite spirit, he will bestow his blessing? We are told that faith—trusting and unfaltering faith—in the power of the Almighty, is sufficient for the removal of mountains—and yet you, because to the eye of human reason your path seems clouded with difficulties, sit down in utter apathy, nor lift up even so much as your voices of prayer, in behalf of a smitten people!

Yet, though there are a fearful number who still listen with a strange indifference to the soul-harrowing eloquence of human suffering, thank heaven! we have no cause of despair. A voice has gone forth over the sleeping pool, to trouble its waters, and there are many who have already gone down and cleansed themselves from the guilt of African oppression.* A spirit is at work among the people that will not easily be quieted—a leaven, whose vital principle will not be destroyed till the whole mass is leavened.

CHARITY

"Though I speak with the tongues of men and of angels," saith St. Paul, "and have not charity, I am become as sounding brass, or a tinkling cymbal. And though I have the gift of prophecy, and understand all mystery, and all knowledge, and though I have all faith so that I could remove mountains, and have not charity, I am nothing. And though I bestow all my goods to feed the poor, and though I give my body to be burned, and have not charity, it profiteth me nothing" [1 Corinthians 13:1–3]. Now as we profess to be a nation of Christians, it is but natural to suppose, that a quality, which appears to be the most essential principle of that religion, should be in good esteem among us, and that the outward form of it, at least, should be held in observance.

But is this the case? We will read you a description of charity, by the same inspired writer, and bid you ask the same question of your consciences. "Charity suffereth long and is kind; charity envieth not; charity vaunteth not itself, is not puffed up, doth not behave unseemly, seeketh not her own, is not easily provoked, thinketh no evil, rejoiceth not in iniquity, but rejoiceth in the truth" [1 Corinthians 13:4–6].

Now which of all these principles does not slavery violate? Where is the long suffering that our slave-holders exhibit, when the most trifling offence on the part of their human cattle is visited by the horsewhip? What is their kindness in claiming from their brethren a daily routine of unmitigated, unrewarded toil, through a long series of years, to feed their luxury? "Charity envieth not"—and truly envy herself could scarcely grudge the few

---

*A reference to the Pool of Siloam in Jerusalem, mentioned in John 9:1–11, reputed to have curative powers whenever its waters stirred.

poor comforts we have left the slave—but is not envy of the superior luxuries and comforts of others, one of the main inducing causes of that oppression?

As for that humility which is so distinguishing a feature in charity and in the Christian religion, we know that it is utterly inconsistent with the very nature of absolute power. Are we not mightily puffed up with our own superiority? Do we not proudly vaunt ourselves as being even of a higher species than our negro brethren? And is it seemly that we should cause oppression with a high hand to rule upon the earth, rioting in the groans of human agony?

Charity seeketh not even that which is her own, but we uphold those who wring with violence from the hands of others that which is not their own. Go ask the poor victim, a female, too, perhaps—who stands there all bleeding and lacerated with many stripes, what was the magnitude of the offence that hath been punished with such severe chastisement—and what will be the answer? Some trifling employment forgotten or neglected—or perhaps the passionate outpourings of grief for some beloved one from whom she has been forcibly separated! Yet will this very text, in the very seat of slavery, be solemnly pronounced from the pulpit, and be characterized as containing some of the sublimest principles of our religion, and commented upon with overpowering eloquence, till the heart of man will glow within his bosom, and the warm tears gush out from the gentle eyes of women—and they will go out from the house of worship, and forget that they are nourishing up within their own households, a system that is at open variance both with that, and every other principle of the Christian religion.

SOURCE: *Essays, Philanthropic and Moral, by Elizabeth Margaret Chandler, Principally Relating to the Abolition of Slavery in America* (Philadelphia: T. E. Chapman, 1845), 12–15.

Declaration of Sentiments (1833)

American Anti-Slavery Society

Founded two years after William Lloyd Garrison began publishing the Liberator, the American Anti-Slavery Society was a powerful force in the abolitionist movement. Like Garrison, its members advocated immediate rather than gradual emancipation of slaves without compensation to their owners. The Society's refusal to compromise was based upon the belief that human bondage was a violation of God's law and that any accommodation to it was therefore sinful. At its initial meeting, the Society adopted this Declaration of Sentiments, authored primarily by Garrison.

The Convention assembled in the city of Philadelphia, to organize a National Anti-Slavery Society, promptly seized the opportunity to promulgate the following Declaration of Sentiments, as cherished by them in relation to the enslavement of one-sixth portion of the American people.

More than fifty-seven years have elapsed, since a band of patriots convened in this place, to devise measures for the deliverance of this country from a foreign yoke. The corner-stone upon which they founded the Temple of Freedom was broadly this— "that all men are created equal; that they are endowed by their Creator with certain inalienable rights; that among these are life, LIBERTY, and the pursuit of happiness." At the sound of their trumpet-call, three millions of people rose up as from the sleep of death, and rushed to the strife of blood; deeming it more glorious to die instantly as freemen, than desirable to live one hour as slaves. They were few in number—poor in resources; but the honest conviction that Truth, Justice and Right were on their side, made them invincible.

We have met together for the achievement of an enterprise, without which that of our fathers is incomplete; and which, for its magnitude, solemnity, and probable results upon the destiny of the world, as far transcends theirs as moral truth does physical force.

In purity of motive, in earnestness of zeal, in decision of purpose, in intrepidity of action, in steadfastness of faith, in sincerity of spirit, we would not be inferior to them.

Their principles led them to wage war against their oppressors, and to spill human blood like water, in order to be free.

Ours forbid the doing of evil that good may come, and lead us to reject, and to entreat the oppressed to reject, the use of all carnal weapons for deliverance from bondage; relying solely upon those which are spiritual, and mighty through God to the pulling down of strong holds.

Their measures were physical resistance—the marshalling in arms—the hostile array—the mortal encounter. Ours shall be such only as the opposition of moral purity to moral corruption—the destruction of error by the potency of truth—the overthrow of prejudice by the power of love—and the abolition of slavery by the spirit of repentance.

Their grievances, great as they were, were trifling in comparison with the wrongs and sufferings of those for whom we plead. Our fathers were never slaves—never bought and sold like cattle —never shut out from the light of knowledge and religion— never subjected to the lash of brutal taskmasters.

But those, for whose emancipation we are striving—constituting at the present time at least one-sixth part of our countrymen—are recognized by law, and treated by their fellow-beings, as marketable commodities, as goods and chattels, as brute beasts; are plundered daily of the fruits of their toil without redress; really enjoy no constitutional nor legal protection from licentious and murderous outrages upon their persons; and are ruthlessly torn asunder—the tender babe from the arms of its frantic mother—the heart-broken wife from her weeping husband—at the caprice or pleasure of irresponsible tyrants. For the crime of having a dark complexion, they suffer the pangs of hunger, the infliction of stripes, the ignominy of brutal servitude. They are kept in heathenish darkness by laws expressly enacted to make their instruction a criminal offence.

These are the prominent circumstances in the condition of more than two millions of our people, the proof of which may be found in thousands of indisputable facts, and in the laws of the slaveholding States.

Hence we maintain—that, in view of the civil and religious privileges of this nation, the guilt of its oppression is unequalled by any other on the face of the earth; and, therefore, that it is bound to repent instantly, to undo the heavy burdens, and to let the oppressed go free.

We further maintain—that no man has a right to enslave or imbrute his brother—to hold or acknowledge him, for one moment, as a piece of merchandise—to keep back his hire by fraud—or to brutalize his mind, by denying him the means of intellectual, social and moral improvement.

The right to enjoy liberty is inalienable. To invade it is to usurp the prerogative of Jehovah. Every man has a right to his own body—to the products of his own labor—to the protection of law—and to the common advantages of society. It is piracy to buy or steal a native African, and subject him to servitude. Surely, the sin is as great to enslave an American as an African.

Therefore we believe and affirm—that there is no difference, in principle, between the African slave trade and American slavery:

That every American citizen, who detains a human being in involuntary bondage as his property, is, according to Scripture, (Ex. xxi. 16) a man-stealer:

That the slaves ought instantly to be set free, and brought under the protection of law:

That if they had lived from the time of Pharaoh down to the present period, and had been entailed through successive generations, their right to be free could never have been alienated, but their claims would have constantly risen in solemnity:

That all those laws which are now in force, admitting the right of slavery, are therefore, before God, utterly null and void; being an audacious usurpation of the Divine prerogative, a daring infringement on the law of nature, a base over-throw of the very foundations of the social compact, a complete extinction of all the relations, endearments and obligations of mankind, and a presumptuous transgression of all the holy commandments; and that therefore they ought instantly to be abrogated.

We further believe and affirm—that all persons of color, who possess the qualifications which are demanded of others, ought to be admitted forthwith to the enjoyment of the same privileges, and the exercise of the same prerogatives, as others; and that the paths of preferment, of wealth, and of intelligence, should be opened as widely to them as to persons of a white complexion.

We maintain that no compensation should be given to the planters emancipating their slaves:

Because it would be a surrender of the great fundamental principle, that man cannot hold property in man:

Because slavery is a crime, and therefore is not an article to be sold:

Because the holders of slaves are not the just proprietors of what they claim; freeing the slave is not depriving them of property, but restoring it to its rightful owner; it is not wronging the master, but righting the slave—restoring him to himself:

Because immediate and general emancipation would only destroy nominal, not real property; it would not amputate a limb or break a bone of the slaves, but by infusing motives into their breasts, would make them doubly valuable to the masters as free laborers; and

Because, if compensation is to be given at all, it should be given to the outraged and guiltless slaves, and not to those who have plundered and abused them.

We regard as delusive, cruel and dangerous, any scheme of expatriation which pretends to aid, either directly or indirectly, in the emancipation of the slaves, or to be a substitute for the immediate and total abolition of slavery.

We fully and unanimously recognize the sovereignty of each State, to legislate exclusively on the subject of the slavery which is tolerated within its limits; we concede that Congress, under the present national compact, has no right to interfere with any of the slave States, in relation to this momentous subject:

But we maintain that Congress has a right, and is solemnly bound, to suppress the domestic slave trade between the several States, and to abolish slavery in those portions of our territory which the Constitution has placed under its exclusive jurisdiction.

We also maintain that there are, at the present time, the highest obligations resting upon the people of the free States to remove slavery by moral and political action, as prescribed in the Constitution of the United States. They are now living under a pledge of their tremendous physical force, to fasten the galling fetters of tyranny upon the limbs of millions in the Southern States; they are liable to be called at any moment to suppress a general insurrection of the slaves; they authorize the slave owner to vote for three-fifths of his slaves as property, and thus enable him to perpetuate his oppression; they support a standing army at the South for its protection and they seize the slave, who has escaped into their territories, and send him back to be tortured by an enraged master or a brutal driver. This relation to slavery is criminal, and full of danger: IT MUST BE BROKEN UP.

These are our views and principles—these our designs and measures. With entire confidence in the overruling justice of God, we plant ourselves upon the Declaration of our Independence and the truths of Divine Revelation, as upon the Everlasting Rock.

We shall organize Anti-Slavery Societies, if possible, in every city, town and village in our land.

We shall send forth agents to lift up the voice of remonstrance, of warning, of entreaty, and of rebuke.

We shall circulate, unsparingly and extensively, anti-slavery tracts and periodicals.

We shall enlist the pulpit and the press in the cause of the suffering and the dumb.

We shalt aim at a purification of the churches from all participation in the guilt of slavery.

We shall encourage the labor of freemen rather than that of slaves, by giving a preference to their productions: and

We shall spare no exertions nor means to bring the whole nation to speedy repentance.

Our trust for victory is solely in God. We may be personally defeated, but our principles never. Truth, Justice, Reason, Humanity, must and will gloriously triumph. Already a host is coming up to the help of the Lord against the mighty, and the prospect before us is full of encouragement.

Submitting this Declaration to the candid examination of the people of this country, and of the friends of liberty throughout the world, we hereby affix our signatures to it; pledging ourselves that, under the guidance and by the help of Almighty God, we will do all that in us lies, consistently with this Declaration of our principles, to overthrow the most execrable system of slavery that has ever been witnessed upon earth; to deliver our land from its deadliest curse; to wipe out the foulest stain which rests upon our national escutcheon; and to secure to the colored population of the United States, all the rights and privileges which belong to them as men, and as Americans—come what may to our persons, our interests, or our reputation—whether we live to witness the triumph of Liberty, Justice and Humanity, or perish untimely as martyrs in this great, benevolent, and holy cause.

SOURCE: Selections from the *Writings and Speeches of William Lloyd Garrison* (Boston: R. F. Wolcut, 1852), 66–72.

LETTERS ON AMERICAN SLAVERY (1833)

JOHN RANKIN

If there was a single book that acquired the status among abolitionists of required reading, it was John Rankin's Letters on American Slavery, *a series of essays addressed to his pro-slavery brother Thomas. William Lloyd Garrison claimed it as a leading inspiration, and Henry Ward Beecher, Congregationalist minister and brother of Harriet Beecher Stowe, author of* Uncle Tom's Cabin, *praised it as an essential force in the struggle to abolish slavery.*

Rankin (1793–1886) was a Presbyterian minister who forsook pulpits in the slave states of Tennessee and Kentucky for one in the free state of Ohio. He settled in Ripley, a town separated from Kentucky by the Ohio River, built himself a home on a high bluff overlooking the river, and displayed lit lanterns every night as beacons for fugitive slaves seeking refuge.

In this selection from his Letters, *Rankin responds to fellow clergyman Archibald Cameron, a slave owner who defended human bondage by appealing to scripture. Cameron argued that the words "servant" and "yoke" in the Bible demonstrated that the apostles endorsed slavery. Rankin counters that Cameron twists their meanings to suit his own purposes. To a casual reader, Rankin's reply may seem an exercise in philological nitpicking. But because the Bible was so frequently invoked to justify slavery, Rankin felt obliged to examine in some detail the meaning of the words Cameron cherry-picked. For a generation that looked to scripture for moral guidance, such clarity was crucial.*

DEAR BROTHER:

I shall in the present letter give you a few remarks upon the arguments which the Rev. Archibald Cameron, of Kentucky, has presented to the public in the first number of the *Monitor*, printed at Lexington, AD 1806. The reverend gentleman possesses both the talents and literature necessary to making the best of the cause he attempts to defend. And could we suppose him actuated by the unhallowed motives of self-interest, we would say he had from that source sufficient inducement to the greatest industry in the management of his subject; for, as we understand, he had, and perhaps still has, considerable property in human flesh, and blood, and souls!! And it became him, as a public teacher, to show, if possible, that his practice was in accordance with the gospel. In short, we believe that if Mr. Cameron had been unsuccessful in adducing arguments to justify the practice of slavery, it was entirely owing to a bad cause, and not to the want of talents, literature or industry.

His arguments are principally drawn from several passages in the New Testament in which servants are mentioned. He lays his strong foundation in the signification of the word *doulos* which is translated into the word servant. He says, "It is well known to those who are in the habit of reading the writings of the ancients, that *doulos* in Greek, the word used above, and *servus* in Latin, are used to signify that kind of servitude which is perpetual or for life, which we call slavery. *Elutheros*, the Greek word for free, is set in opposition to *doulos*, servant, which shows that the Apostle meant a bondman, or a slave, when he used the term."

This argument is plausible, but not solid. Paul says, "Though I be (*elutheros*) free from all men, yet I have made myself (*edoulosa*) servant unto all." (1 Cor. ix. 19.) And he commands the Galatians (*douleuete*) to serve one another by love. (Gal. v. 13.) *Edoulosa* signifies I have made myself (*doulos*) a servant; and is set in opposition to (*Elutheros*) free; but who would argue from this that Paul was an involuntary slave for life?

Yet such an argument would be just as conclusive as the one which Mr. Cameron has advanced in the passage we have quoted from the *Monitor*. I readily admit that the apostle had reference to some kind of servitude when he said, "Art thou called, being (*doulos*) a servant, care not for it; but if thou mayest be made (*elutheros*) free, use it rather." (1 Cor. vii. 21.) But there is no evidence from the language of the text what kind of servitude was meant. The Greek word *doulos*, like the English word servant, specifies no particular kind of servitude. Hence the translators have not, in a single instance, in all the New Testament, translated the word *doulos* into the word slave.

The word slave is specific in its meaning, and always, except when used figuratively, denotes one bound to involuntary and perpetual servitude; and in all its more general applications, it still refers to one particular kind of bondage. Every slave is a servant, but every servant is not a slave. All apprentices are servants, and actually bondmen during their apprenticeship, and are, in many instances, subjected to stripes; but they are not called slaves. Hirelings are servants, and in some parts of the world even these have endured slaves; yet no accurate writer would call them slaves.

The translators thought it proper to use the word slave in but a single instance, in all the New Testament. (Rev. xviii. 13.) "Slaves and souls of men" are mentioned as the unhallowed merchandise of spiritual Babylon. And here the Greek word is not *doulos* but *somaton*, the genitive plural of *soma*.

The truth is, the word *doulos* has such an extensive and various application in the sacred scriptures, that it would be very injudicious to translate it into a word so limited and determinate in its signification as is the word slave, which properly denotes a person bound to involuntary and perpetual servitude.

Doulos has no such definitive meaning, but answers to the English word servant, which is as applicable to the subject of a prince, to the common hireling, or even to the apprentice, as it is to the slave. In many instances it would be most ridiculous to translate *doulos* into slave, as a single specification will show. 'Paul (*doulos*) a slave of Jesus Christ.' How ridiculous is such a translation!

Christ is "The Prince of the Kings of the earth." Paul is his servant, but not his involuntary slave.

Doulos is used in relation to the subjects of kings or nobles. (Luke xix. 17.) "Well, thou good (*doule*) servant—have thou authority over ten cities." Certainly the subject of a prince, and not a slave, must have been intended by *doule* in this passage. Who would imagine that authority over ten cities would be given to a slave?

Doulos is likewise used in relation to hired servants. The penitent prodigal said, "How many (*misthioi*) hirelings, or hired servants of my father's have bread enough." And again, when expressing his willingness to accept the lowest station in his father's house, he said, 'I am no more worthy to be called thy son: make me as one of thy hired servants." But the father said to his (*doulos*) servants, bring forth the best robe and put it on him. (Luke, xv. 11–32.) The prodigal said that the hirelings were his father's, and had bread enough and to spare. This would be quite unnatural, if there were still a lower order of servants in his father's house, and indeed would imply that such servants had not bread enough.

Again, he says, make me as one of thy hirelings. This, on the supposition that there were still lower order than these in his father's family, was as good as saying, I am not yet unworthy enough to take the lowest place in thy family; and would destroy both the beauty and fitness of the parable, which was intended to illustrate the nature of true repentance, and the willingness of our heavenly Father to receive the humble penitent. The truly penitent sinner is willing to take the lowest station in his father's house.

But Mr. Cameron, contrary to the nature of the parable, supposes that the father of the prodigal held slaves; but upon such supposition the prodigal was very unlike the penitent sinner whom he was intended to represent. Hence it is evident that the father's (*douloi*) servants were his hirelings. Once more, *doulos* is used in relation to such as dedicate themselves to the service of others. So Paul, as we have already shown, made himself (*doulos*) a servant unto all. And so those who have dedicated themselves to the service of God are called his servants. (Rev. xxii. 3.) "And his (*douloi*) servants shall serve him."

The elder brother of the prodigal is represented as saying to his father, "Lo, these many years (*doulueo*) do I serve thee!" And our Lord says, "Whosoever commiteth sin, is the (*doulos*) servant of sin." (John viii. 34.) Paul also says, "To whom ye yield yourselves (*douloi*) servants to obey, his (*douloi*) servants ye are." (Rom. vi. 16.)

Consequently, Mr. Cameron must be mistaken when he says, "that *doulos* in Greek—is used to signify that kind of servitude which is perpetual for life, which we call slavery." It has no such definite signification; no difference whether a man serves voluntarily or involuntarily, whether he serves an hour or during life, he is (*doulos*) a servant during the time he serves. It is a general term which is equally applicable to all kinds of servants, without regard either to the nature or duration of their servitude. Hence, it affords no proof either for or against our present system of slavery. Thus far we think Mr. Cameron has failed in his arguments.

Again, Mr. Cameron quoted 1 Tim. vi. 1, 2: "Let as many servants as are under the yoke, count their own masters worthy of all honor; that the name of God and his doctrine be not blasphemed. And they that have believing masters, let them not despise them because they are brethren; but rather do them service because they are faithful and beloved partakers of the benefit."

He appears to be confident "that this has a reference to slavery, or perpetual servitude."

And in connection with it, he tells us of an ancient custom of making captives pass under the yoke as a token of their subjection to slavery, that such "Were sold and bought like other property," and that of this description of persons the Apostle Paul says, "Let as many servants as are (*upozugon*) under the yoke, count their own masters worthy of all honor." But I see not the least evidence that the apostle had any reference to such custom.

The apostle does not say, let as many servants as have passed under the yoke; but he says, "Let as many servants as are under the yoke, count their own masters worthy of all honor." The yoke which he mentions is not one under which they had passed; but one that was still upon them.

And according to Mr. Cameron's own description of the instrument under which captives were made to pass, it is evident that the apostle had no reference to it as an emblem of perpetual slavery.

In a note on the word yoke he says, "*Jugum*, a yoke, a contrivance with forks and spears, like a gallows, under which enemies vanquished were forced to go. Hence it is used to signify bondage or slavery."

But *zugon*, the word which the apostle uses, signifies no such kind of yoke as Mr. Cameron here describes; it is derived from the Greek verb *zeugnuo* (I join together,) and consequently signifies an instrument of conjugation, such as the yoke which unites or couples oxen together; and because it thus couples them, it is called *zugon* (a yoke); therefore, it is not the kind of instrument under which Mr. Cameron says captives were made to pass as an emblem of their being subjected to slavery.

In allusion to the yoke which binds the ox to his fellow, bondage of various kinds is in the scriptures termed a yoke. Subjects are bound to obey their prince, and thus are under the yoke. (1 Kings xii. 4.) Christ is a king, and they that will be his subjects must take his yoke upon them—"Take my yoke upon you, for my yoke is easy." (Matt. xi. 29, 30.)

Again, the husband is bound to the wife, and the wife to the husband; and though they are thus bound by voluntary engagement, and though their union be a source of their greatest happiness, yet they are under the yoke. Hence, Paul says (2 Cor. vi. 14), "Be ye not unequally yoked together." (Phil. iv. 3.) "I entreat thee, also, true yoke fellow." This was a certain person who had voluntarily associated himself with Paul in propagating the gospel among the heathen.

These instances are sufficient to show that the word yoke is figuratively used as a general term, which is equally applicable to every kind of bondage. Mr. Cameron himself admits that every "obligation to virtue" is a yoke. He there argues that "If the phrase every yoke, be not qualified and restricted, it will be proper to break asunder the yoke of Christianity, the yoke of the civil law, the yoke of marriage, and every other obligation to virtue." Thus while he pleads for a limitation of the phrase "every yoke," he admits the universal application of the term yoke in respect to every "obligation to virtue." It is strange that he makes such admission, after limiting the term to perpetual and involuntary slavery.

But what is still more strange, he first argues that the term yoke is applicable to slavery alone, when used by the Apostle in relation to servants; but when he is commanded to "break every yoke," (Isa 58) he argues that the phrase "every yoke" must be so "qualified and restricted" as not to include slavery; else he says, "It will be proper to break asunder the yoke of Christianity, the yoke of civil law, the yoke of marriage, and every other obligation to virtue."

If the phrase "every yoke" does not include slavery, I do not see how the phrase "under the yoke" can signify slavery.

That the apostle Paul had reference to some kind of bondage when he used the phrase "under the yoke," I readily admit; but I see no evidence that he had reference to involuntary and perpetual slavery. Hired servants were in that age very numerous. The father of the prodigal is represented as having many of them in his service. The prodigal says, "How many hired servants of my father's have bread enough!" And the Apostle James in his epistle severely reproves the rich for defrauding the laborers that had reaped their fields. (James v. 4.) "Behold, the hire of the laborers who have reaped down your fields, which is of you kept back by fraud, crieth, and the cries of them which have reaped are entered into the ears of the Lord of Sabaoth." This shows that the fields of the rich were generally reaped by hired servants, and not by slaves.

Now, had slaves been so exceedingly numerous as Mr. Cameron attempts, by profane history, to prove them to have been, the rich would have no need to hire reapers. If slaves were held, they were held by the rich; but James, in a general epistle intended for the use of all the churches, represents the rich as hiring their reapers. This does not evidence that slaves were numerous.

But had the rich generally held slaves, and treated them with so shocking cruelty as Mr. Cameron says they did, can we suppose that the agonizing cries of the poor slaves would not have "entered into the ears of the Lord of Sabaoth," as well as the cries of defrauded hirelings? Has the Almighty no compassion for the hapless slave? Surely the Sovereign of the universe is no respecter of persons, his compassion descends to the meanest of his creatures; the angel and the worm are alike the subjects of his care. Hence it is most reasonable to conclude, that had there been suffering slaves in the hands of the rich, their cries must have been heard in Heaven, and also regarded in the denunciations delivered by the inspired apostle.

Persons who were in a state of abject poverty were under the necessity of devoting themselves to the service of the rich for wages, and that in many instances, during the space of several years together; and when they entered into a contract of such duration, they were bound to fulfil the term of service if required; and thus they were under the yoke; and when they bound themselves to the service of ill-disposed masters it became a grievous yoke; but, nevertheless, they were generally obliged to bear it until their term of service was completed according to agreement.

Some in consequence of being in debt sold themselves for a limited time in order to make payment; other insolvent debtors might be sold by their creditors; and we may suppose some sold for crime. In addition to these, we may also suppose that many were bound as apprentices.

All these several classes were under the yoke during the time for which they were bound to service; and therefore might be properly addressed in the language of Paul. "Let as many servants as are under the yoke count their own masters worthy of all honor, that the name of God and his doctrine be not blasphemed. And they that have believing masters, let them not despise them."

That the apostle addressed servants, and not slaves, appears evident when we consider that God long before positively prohibited the enslaving of his people, and with the prohibition he assigned the reason on which it was founded: "They are my servants." This reason must stand alike good in every age, and ever prohibit Christians from enslaving their brethren. "But over your brethren—ye shall not rule—with rigor." "For they are my servants." (Lev. xxv. 42, 46.)

I cannot believe that the apostle under the inspiration of the Holy Spirit did, in opposition to this positive command, permit Christians to hold their brethren as slaves for life, and also to have the power of selling both them and their offspring as mere property! But it would be proper for the several classes of servants we have mentioned to fulfil their terms, and render the service due to their own masters, whether Christian or heathen. And to the heathen they ought to be both faithful and respectful, lest they should cause them to say that Christianity made their servants dishonest, or unwilling to render them such service and regard as were justly due.

And love to their Christian masters, who were faithful and beloved brethren, ought to induce them to render them still more willingly the service and honor which were justly due; and thus while fulfilling their just obligations, they would be doing good to their brethren, and so would enable them to extend their liberality to those who were propagating the gospel. And I do not see why all the addresses made to servants in the apostolic epistles might not be applicable to persons bound to servitude for a limited time. Such as were bound to intolerant heathen might endure great evils; in such cases it would be desirable to be liberated by satisfying the master in some lawful way for the service due him. And, perhaps it was on this account that Paul said, "Art thou called, being a servant, care not for it; but if thou mayest be free, use it rather."

But when this could not be obtained in an equitable manner, it would be their duty to serve even the forward as well as the gentle—it was such service as justice required; hence, it was proper to enjoin obedience upon them. "Servants, obey in all things your masters according to the flesh; not with eye-service, as men-pleasers, but in singleness of heart fearing God." (Col. iii. 22.) This plainly implies that the service was justly due; and that, therefore, it should be rendered in the fear of God, who would punish them in case they should defraud their masters. And these same masters were commanded to give unto their servants whatever wages were due for their services. "Masters, give unto your servants that which is just and equate." (Col. iv. 1.)

But in some instances, reference is made to the stripes which servants endured. And from this Mr. Cameron concludes such servants were slaves for life; but many who were servants for a limited time have endured stripes. Hence, enduring stripes is no certain proof of the existence of perpetual slavery.

Again Mr. Cameron attempts to prove by the Greek phrase *o pais mou* that the Centurion's servant whom our Lord healed was a slave born in his family; but the word *pais* is sometimes used as *doulos*, a servant. (Luke, i. 54.) "He hath helped his servant Israel." (Luke xv. 20.) "And he called one of the servants." *Pais* is used in both those passages to signify servant. Hence the phrase, *o pais mou*, signifies 'my servant,' just as it is expressed in our translation. (Luke, vii. 7.) Therefore it has no reference to the servant being born in the Centurion's family, nor does it afford any evidence that he was a slave for life.

I have now considered the principal arguments which Mr. Cameron has adduced to prove that the apostles did permit the primitive Christians to hold slaves; and though I readily grant that they are the test his cause will admit, yet I do not think them sufficient to establish his point, or to justify his practice of holding as property his fellow men. I am fully persuaded that a point so unreasonable, and a practice so unjust, can never find support from the sacred volume.

I have now completed my examination of the principal arguments which the abettors of slavery have drawn from the scriptures in order to support our modern system of cruel oppression. ADIEU.

SOURCE: John Rankin, *Letters on American Slavery, Addressed to Mr. Thomas Rankin*. 2nd edition. (Newburyport, MA: Charles Whipple, 1836), 90–101.

PART THREE

THE ANTEBELLUM PERIOD

Christ vs. the Slavocracy

An Appeal to
the Christian Women of the South (1836)

Angelina Grimké

Along with her older sister Sarah, Angelina Grimké (1805–1879) was a southern-born Quaker who became a staunch opponent of slavery and advocate of abolitionism. Like so many other female abolitionists, she was an equally outspoken champion of women's rights after the Civil War ended legal human bondage in the States.

In this selection from her influential address to southern women slaveholders, Grimké responds to an argument frequently invoked by Christian proponents of slavery, that there's no evidence in the Bible of Jesus condemning the institution, and appeals to the Golden Rule. She then goes on to reject the equally spurious argument that bondage isn't as onerous to a black person as it would be to a white one, and concludes with counsel on how women, relatively unempowered in early nineteenth-century America, can exert influence in the struggle for abolition.

It is because I feel a deep and tender interest in your present and eternal welfare that I am willing thus publicly to address you. Some of you have loved me as a relative, and some have felt bound to me in Christian sympathy, and Gospel fellowship; and even when compelled by a strong sense of duty, to break those outward bonds of union which bound us together as members of the same community, and members of the same religious denomination, you were generous enough to give me credit, for sincerity as a Christian, though you believed I had been most strangely deceived. I thanked you then for your kindness, and I ask you *now*, for the sake of former confidence and former friendship, to read the following pages in the spirit of calm investigation and fervent prayer. It is because you have known me, that I write thus unto you.

But there are other Christian women scattered over the Southern States, a very large number of whom have never seen me, and never heard my name, and who feel *no* interest whatever in *me*. But I feel an interest in *you*, as branches of the same vine from whose root I daily draw the principle of spiritual vitality— Yes! Sisters in Christ I feel an interest in *you*, and often has the secret prayer arisen on your behalf, Lord "open thou their eyes that they may see wondrous things out of thy Law"—It is then, because I *do feel* and *do pray* for you, that I thus address you upon a subject about which of all others, perhaps you would rather not hear any thing; but, "would to God ye could bear with me a little in my folly, and indeed bear with me, for I am jealous over you with godly jealousy." Be not afraid then to read my appeal; it is *not* written in the heat of passion or prejudice, but in that solemn calmness which is the result of conviction and duty. It is true, I am going to tell you unwelcome truths, but I mean to speak those *truths in love*, and remember Solomon says, "faithful are the *wounds* of a friend." I do not believe the time has yet come when *Christian women* "will not endure sound doctrine," even on the subject of Slavery, if it is spoken to them in tenderness and love, therefore I now address you....

Some have even said that Jesus Christ did not condemn slavery. To this I reply, that our Holy Redeemer lived and preached among the Jews only. That he saw nothing of perpetual servitude is certain from the simple declaration made by himself in John 8:35: "The servant abideth not in the house for ever, the son abideth ever." If then he did not condemn Jewish temporary servitude, this does not prove that he would not have condemned such a monstrous system as that of AMERICAN slavery, if that had existed among them. But did not Jesus condemn slavery? Let us examine some of his precepts. "Whatsoever ye would that men should do to you, do ye even so to them." Let every slaveholder apply these queries to his own heart: Am I willing to be a slave—Am I willing to see my husband the slave of another—Am I willing to see my mother a slave, or my father, my white sister, or my white brother? If not, then in holding others as slaves, I am doing what I would not wish to be done to me or any relative I have; and thus have I broken this golden rule which was given me to walk by.

But some shareholders have said, "we were never in bondage to any man," and therefore the yoke of bondage would be insufferable to us, but slaves are accustomed to it, their backs are fitted to the burden. Well, I am willing to admit that you who have lived in freedom would find slavery even more oppressive than the poor slave does, but then you may try this question in another form—Am I willing to reduce my little child to slavery? You know that if it is brought up a slave, it will never know any contrast between freedom and bondage; its back will become fitted to the burden just as the negro child's does—*not by nature*—but by daily, violent pressure, in the same way that the head of the Indian child becomes flattened by the boards in which it is bound. It has been justly remarked that "God never made a slave," he made man upright; his back was not made to carry burdens as the slave of another, nor his neck to wear a yoke, and the man must be crushed within him, before his back can be fitted to the burden of perpetual slavery; and that his back is not fitted to it, is manifest by the insurrections that so often disturb the peace and security of slaveholding countries. Who ever heard of a rebellion of the beasts of the field?...

But perhaps you will be ready to query, why appeal to *women* on this subject? We do not make the laws which perpetuate slavery. No legislative power is vested in us; *we* can do nothing to overthrow the system, even if we wished to do so. To this I reply, I know you do not make the laws, but I also know that you *are the wives and mothers, the sisters and daughters of those who do*; and if you really suppose you can do nothing to overthrow slavery, you are greatly mistaken. You can do much in every way: four things I will name. 1st. You can read on this subject. 2d. You can pray over this subject. 3d. You can speak on this subject. 4th. You can *act* on this subject. I have not placed reading before praying because I regard it more important, but because, in order to pray aright, we must understand what we are praying for; it is only then we can "pray with the understanding, and the spirit also."

1. Read then on the subject of slavery. Search the Scriptures daily, whether the things I have told you are true. Other books and papers might be a great help to you in this investigation, but they are not necessary, and it is hardly probable that your Committees of Vigilance will allow you to have any other. The *Bible* then is the book I want you to read in the spirit of inquiry, and the spirit of prayer. Even the enemies of Abolitionists, acknowledge that their doctrines are drawn from it. In the great mob in Boston, last autumn, when the books and papers of the Anti-Slavery Society, were thrown out of the windows of their office, one individual laid hold of the Bible and was about tossing it out to the ground, when another reminded him that it was the Bible he had in his hand. "O! *'tis all one*," he replied, and out went the sacred volume, along with the rest. We thank him for the acknowledgment. Yes, "*it is all one*," for our books and papers are mostly commentaries on the Bible, and the Declaration. Read the *Bible* then, it contains the words *of* Jesus, and they are spirit and life. Judge for yourselves whether *he sanctioned* such a system of oppression and crime.

2. Pray over this subject. When you have entered into your closets, and shut to the doors, then pray to your father, who seeth in secret, that he would open your eyes to see whether slavery is sinful, and if it is, that he would enable you to bear a faithful, open and unshrinking testimony against it, and to do whatsoever your hands find to do, leaving the consequences entirely to him, who still says to us whenever we try to reason away duty from the fear of consequences, "*What is that to thee, follow thou me.*" Pray also

for that poor slave, that he may be kept patient and submissive under his hard lot, until God is pleased to open the door of freedom to him without violence or bloodshed. Pray too for the master that his heart may be softened, and he made willing to acknowledge, as Joseph's brethren did, "Verily we are guilty concerning our brother," before he will be compelled to add in consequence of Divine judgment, "therefore is all this evil come upon us." Pray also for all your brethren and sisters who are laboring in the righteous cause of Emancipation in the Northern States, England and the world. There is great encouragement for prayer in these words of our Lord. "Whatsoever ye shall ask the Father in my *name*, he will *give* it to you"—Pray then without ceasing, in the closet and the social circle.

3. Speak on this subject. It is through the tongue, the pen, and the press, that truth is principally propagated. Speak then to your relatives, your friends, your acquaintances on the subject of slavery; be not afraid if you are conscientiously convinced it is *sinful*, to say so openly, but calmly, and to let your sentiments be known. If you are served by the slaves of others, try to ameliorate their condition as much as possible; never aggravate their faults, and thus add fuel to the fire of anger already kindled, in a master and mistress's bosom; remember their extreme ignorance, and consider them as your Heavenly Father does the less culpable on this account, even when they do wrong things. Discountenance all cruelty to them, all starvation, all corporal chastisement; these may brutalize and break their spirits, but will never bend them to willing, cheerful obedience. If possible, see that they are comfortably and seasonably fed, whether in the house or the field; it is unreasonable and cruel to expect slaves to wait for their breakfast until eleven o'clock, when they rise at five or six. Do all you can, to induce their owners to clothe them well, and to allow them many little indulgences which would contribute to their comfort. Above all, try to persuade your husband, father, brothers and sons, that slavery is a crime against God and man, and that it is

a great sin to keep human beings in such abject ignorance; to deny them the privilege of learning to read and write. The Catholics are universally condemned, for denying the Bible to the common people, but, slaveholders must not blame them, for they are doing the very same thing, and for the very same reason, neither of these systems can bear the light which bursts from the pages of that Holy Book. And lastly, endeavor to inculcate submission on the part of the slaves, but whilst doing this be faithful in pleading the cause of the oppressed.

> Will you behold unheeding,
> Life's holiest feelings crushed,
> Where *woman's* heart is bleeding,
> Shall *woman's* voice be hushed?*

4. Act on this subject. Some of you own slaves yourselves. If you believe slavery is sinful, set them at liberty, "undo the heavy burdens and let the oppressed go free." If they wish to remain with you, pay them wages, if not let them leave you. Should they remain teach them, and have them taught the common branches of an English education; they have minds and those minds ought to be improved. So precious a talent as intellect, never was given to be wrapt in a napkin and buried in the earth. It is the duty of all, as far as they can, to improve their own mental faculties, because we are commanded to love God with all our minds, as well as with all our hearts, and we commit a great sin, if we forbid or prevent that cultivation of the mind in others, which would enable them to perform this duty. Teach your servants then to read &c, and encourage them to believe it is their duty to learn, if it were only that they might read the Bible.

SOURCE: Angelina Grimké, *Appeal to the Christian Women of the South* (New York: American Anti-Slavery Society, 1836), 1–2, 12, 16–18.

---

*A stanza from a popular anti-slavery hymn.

An Epistle to
the Clergy of the Southern States (1836)

Sarah Moore Grimké

*There are few abolitionist documents more breathtakingly audacious
than Sarah Grimké's (1792–1873) admonition to southern clergy who
defend slavery. Eloquently written and decisively argued, her pamphlet
infuriated ministers and laypersons alike in slave states—how presumptuous of a mere lay woman to lecture them on their Christian
duty!—and there were several public burnings of it.*

*Grimké argues that when it comes to slaves, slavery-endorsing
clergy collapse the biblical distinction between humans, made in God's
image, and nonhuman objects, thereby relegating slaves to the moral
status of thinghood. In doing so, they think they are serving God but
in fact are seduced by Satan. Consequently, their preaching is a thinly
veiled advocacy of the "kingdom of darkness." Grimké urges the clergy
to repent, warning them that no one can know the moment of Christ's
return, and recommends immediate rather than gradual emancipation
as a first step in their return to Christian principles.*

It is because I feel a portion of that love glowing in my heart towards you, which is infused into every bosom by the cordial re-
ception of the gospel of Jesus Christ, that I am induced to address
you as fellow professors of his holy religion. . . .

A solemn sense of the duty which I owe as a Southerner to
every class of the community of which I was once a part, likewise
impels me to address you, especially, who are filling the important

and responsible station of ministers of Jehovah, expounders of
the lively oracles of God. It is because you sway the minds of a
vast proportion of the Christian community, who regard you as
the channel through which divine knowledge must flow. Nor
does the fact that you are voluntarily invested by the people with
this high prerogative, lessen the fearful weight of responsibility
which attaches to you as watchmen on the walls of Zion. It adds
rather a tenfold weight of guilt, because the very first duty which
devolves upon you is to teach them not to trust in man. —Oh my
brethren, is this duty faithfully performed? Is not the idea inculcated that to you they must look for the right understanding of
the sacred volume, and has not your interpretation of the Word
of God induced thousands and tens of thousands to receive as
truth, sanctioned by the authority of Heaven, the oft repeated
declaration that slavery, American slavery, stamped as it is with
all its infinity of horrors, bears upon it the signet of that God
whose name is Love?

Let us contemplate the magnificent scene of creation, when
God looked upon chaos and said, "Let there be light, and there
was light" [Genesis 1:3]. The dark abyss was instantaneously illu-
minated, and a flood of splendor poured upon the face of the
deep, and "God saw the light that it was good" [Genesis 1:4]. Behold the work of creation carried on and perfected—the azure sky
and verdant grass, the trees, the beasts, the fowls of the air, and
whatsoever passeth through the paths of the sea, the greater light
to rule the day, the lesser light to rule the night, and all the starry
host of heaven, brought into existence by the simple command,
Let them be.

But was man, the lord of this creation, thus ushered into
being? No, the Almighty, clothed as he is with all power in
heaven and in earth, paused when he had thus far completed his
glorious work—"Omnipotence retired, if I may so speak, and held
a counsel when he was about to place upon the earth the
sceptered monarch of the universe." He did not say let man be,
but "Let us make man in our image, after our likeness, and let

them have dominion over the fish of the sea, and over the fowl of the air,—and over the cattle, and over all the earth, and over every creeping thing, that creepeth upon the earth" [Genesis 1:26]. Here is written in characters of fire continually blazing before the eyes of every man who holds his fellow man in bondage—In the image of God created he man. Here is marked a distinction which can never be effaced between a man and *a thing*, and we are fighting against God's unchangeable decree by depriving this rational and immortal being of those inalienable rights which have been conferred upon him. He was created a little lower than the angels, crowned with glory and honor, and designed to be God's viceregent upon earth—but slavery has wrested the sceptre of dominion from his hand, slavery has seized with an iron grasp this God-like being, and torn the crown from his head. Slavery has disrobed him of royalty, put on him the collar and the chain, and trampled the image of God in the dust.

> Eternal God! when from thy giant hand,
> Thou heaved the floods, and fixed the trembling land:
> When life sprung startling at thy plastic call;
> Endless her forms, and man the Lord of all—
> Say, was that lordly form, inspired by thee,
> To wear eternal chains and bow the knee?
> Was man ordained the slave of man to toil,
> Yoked with the brutes and fettered to the soil?*

This, my brethren, is slavery—this is what sublimates the atrocity of that act, which virtually says, I will as far as I am able destroy the image of God, blot him from creation as a man, and convert him into a thing—"a chattel personal." Can any crime, tremendous as is the history of human wickedness, compare in

---

*From Thomas Campbell's "Pleasures of Hope." Grimké has changed Campbell's original "Eternal Nature!" to "Eternal God!"

turpitude with this?—No, the immutable difference, the *heaven-wide distinction* which God has established between *that* being whom he has made a little lower than the angels, and all the other works of this wonderful creation, cannot be annihilated without incurring a weight of guilt beyond expression terrible....

The present position of my country and of the church is one of deep and solemn interest. The times of our ignorance on the subject of slavery which God may have winked at, *have passed away*. We are no longer standing unconsciously and carelessly on the brink of a burning volcano. The strong arm of Almighty power has rolled back the dense cloud which hung over the terrific crater, and has exposed it to our view, and although no human eye can penetrate the abyss, yet enough is seen to warn us of the consequences of trifling with Omnipotence. Jehovah is calling to us as he did to Job out of the whirlwind, and every blast bears on its wings the sound, Repent! Repent! God, if I may so speak, is waiting to see whether we will hearken unto his voice. He has sent out his light and his truth, and as regards us it may perhaps be said—there is now silence in heaven. The commissioned messengers of grace to this guilty nation are rapidly traversing our country, through the medium of the Anti-Slavery Society, through its agents and its presses, whilst the "ministering spirits" are marking with breathless interest the influence produced by these means of knowledge thus mercifully furnished to our land. Oh! if there be joy in heaven over one sinner that repenteth, what hallelujahs of angelic praise will arise, when the slave-holder and the defender of slavery bow before the footstool of mercy, and with broken spirits and contrite hearts surrender unto God that dominion over his immortal creatures which he alone can rightly exercise.

What an appalling spectacle do we now present! With one hand we clasp the cross of Christ, and with the other grasp the neck of the down-trodden slave! With one eye we are gazing imploringly on the bleeding sacrifice of Calvary, as if we expected redemption though the blood which was shed there, and with the other we cast the glance of indignation and contempt at the representative of Him who there, made his soul an offering for sin! My Christian brethren, if there is any truth in the Bible, and in the God of the Bible, *our hearts bear us witness* that he can no more acknowledge us as his disciples, if we willfully persist in this sin, than he did the Pharisees formerly, who were strict and punctilious in the observance of the ceremonial law, and yet devoured widows' houses. *We have added a deeper shade to their guilt*, we make widows by tearing from the victims of a cruel bondage, the husbands of their bosoms, and then devour the widow herself by robbing her of her freedom, and reducing her to the level of a brute. I solemnly appeal to your own consciences. Does not the rebuke of Christ to the Pharisees apply to some of those who are exercising the office of Gospel ministers, "Woe unto you, Scribes and Pharisees, hypocrites! for ye devour widow's houses, and for a pretense make long prayers, therefore ye shall receive the greater damnation" [Matthew 23:14].

How long the space now granted for repentance may continue, is among the secret things which belong unto God, and my soul ardently desires that all those who are enlisted in the ranks of abolition may regard every day as possibly the last, and may pray without ceasing to God, to grant this nation repentance and forgiveness of the sin of slavery. The time is precious, unspeakably precious, and every encouragement is offered to us to supplicate the God of the master and of the slave to make a "right way" for us, and for our little ones, and for all our substance." Ezra says, "so we fasted and besought the Lord, and he was entreated for us" [Ezra 8:23]. Look at the marvelous effects of prayer when Peter was imprisoned. What did the church in that crisis? She felt that her weapons were not carnal, but spiritual, and "prayer was made without ceasing" [1 Thessalonians 5:17]. These petitions offered in humble faith were mighty through God to the emancipation of Peter. "Is the Lord's arm shortened that it cannot save, or his ear grown heavy that it cannot hear?" [Isaiah 59:1]. If he condescended to work a miracle in answer to prayer when one of his servants was imprisoned, will he not graciously hear our supplications when two millions of his immortal creatures are in bondage? We entreat the Christian ministry to co-operate with us to unite in our petitions to Almighty God to deliver our land from blood guiltiness; to enable us to see the abominations of American slavery by the light of the gospel. "This is the condemnation, that light is come into the world, but men loved darkness rather than light, because their deeds were evil" [John 3:19]. Then may we expect a glorious consummation to our united labors of love. Then may the Lord Jesus unto whom belongeth all power in heaven and in earth condescend to answer our prayers, and by the softening influence of his holy spirit induce our brethren and sisters of the South "to undo the heavy burdens, to break every yoke and let the oppressed go free" [Isaiah 58:6]. . . .

Oh, my brethren! when you are telling to an admiring audience that through your instrumentality nearly two millions of Bibles and Testaments have been disseminated throughout the world, does not the voice of the slave vibrate on your ear, as it floats over the sultry plains of the South, and utters forth his lamentation, "Hast thou, but one blessing, my father? *Bless me, even me also*, O my father!" [Genesis 27:38]. Does no wail of torment interrupt the eloquent harangue?—And from the bottomless pit does no accusing voice arise to charge you with the perdition of those seals from whom you wrested, as far as you were able, the power of working out their own salvation?

Our country, I believe, has arrived at an awful crisis. God has in infinite mercy raised up those who have moral courage and religion enough to obey the divine command, "Cry aloud and spare not, lift up thy voice like a trumpet, and show my people their transgressions" [Isaiah 58:1]—Our sins are set in order before us, and we are now hesitating whether we shall choose the curse pronounced by Jehovah, "Cursed be he that perverteth the judgment of the stranger, fatherless and widow" [Deuteronomy 27:19] or the blessing recorded in the 41st Psl. " Blessed is the man that considereth the poor (or the weak), the Lord will deliver him in the time of trouble.". . .

If then there be, as I humbly trust there are among my Christian brethren some who like the prophet of old are ready to exclaim! "Woe is me for I am undone; because I am a man of unclean lips; for mine eyes have seen the King, the Lord of Hosts" [Isaiah 6:5]—If to some of you Jehovah has unveiled the abominations of American Slavery, the guilt of yourselves and of your brethren! Oh remember the prophet of Israel and be encouraged. Your lips like his will be touched with a live coal from off the altar. The Lord will be your light and your salvation: He will go before you and the God of Israel will be your reward.

If ever there was a time when the Church of Christ was called upon to make an *aggressive* movement on the kingdom of darkness, *this is the time*. The subject of slavery is fairly before the American public.—The consciences of the slave-holders at the South and of their coadjutors at the North are aroused, notwithstanding all the opiates which are so abundantly administered under the plea of necessity, and expediency, and the duty of obedience to man, rather than to God. In regard to slavery, Satan has transformed himself into an angel of light, and under the false pretense of consulting the good of the slaves, pleads for retaining them in bondage, until they are prepared to enjoy the blessings of liberty. Full well he knows that if he can but gain time, he gains everything. When he stood beside Felix and saw that he trembled before his fettered captive, as Paul reasoned of righteousness, temperance, and judgment to come, he summoned to his aid this masterpiece of Satanic ingenuity, and whispered, say to this Apostle, "Go thy way for this time, at a more convenient season, I will call for thee" [Acts 24:25]. The heart of Felix responded to this intimation, and his lips uttered the fatal words—fatal, because, for aught that appears, they sealed his death warrant for eternity. Let me appeal to every Christian minister, who has known what it is to repent and forsake his sins: Have you not all found that prospective repentance and future amendment are destruction to the soul? The truth is, to postpone present duty, to get ready for the discharge of future, is just putting yourselves into the hands of Satan to prepare you for the service of God. Just so, gradualism puts the slave into the hands of his master, whose interest it is to keep him enslaved, to prepare him for freedom, because that master says at a convenient season I will liberate my captive. So says the adversary of all good, serve me today and tomorrow thou mayest serve God. Oh lay not this flattering unction to your souls, ye that are teachers in Israel. God is not mocked, and ye may as well expect indulgence in sin to purify the heart and prepare the soul for an inheritance with the saints in light, as to suppose that slavery can fit men for freedom. That which debases and brutalizes can never fit for freedom. The chains of the slave must be sundered; he must be taught that he is heaven-born and destined to the skies again, he must be restored to his dignified station in the scale of creation, he must be crowned again with the diadem of glory, again ranked amongst the sons of God and invested with lordly prerogative over every living creature. If you would aid in this mighty, this glorious achievement—Preach the word of Immediate Emancipation.

SOURCE: Sarah Grimké, *An Epistle to the Clergy of the Southern States* (Boston: n.p., 1836), 1, 2–3, 10–11, 13, 14–15, 16.

The Bible Against Slavery (1837)

Theodore Dwight Weld

Husband to Angelina Grimké, Theodore Weld (1803–1895) co-authored with her and Sarah Grimké a collection of firsthand accounts of slavery, American Slavery As It Is *(1839), which served as an inspiration for Harriet Beecher Stowe's* Uncle Tom's Cabin. *Two years earlier, perhaps inspired by Sarah Grimké's claim that human bondage reduced slaves to the moral status of things, he had written* The Bible Against Slavery, *a title with a deliberate double entendre.*

In it, Weld goes to some pains to distinguish between certain kinds of voluntary or involuntary servitude—apprenticeships and imprisonments, for example—and slavery. The latter's distinctively tragic characteristic is that it "unseats a man to make room for a thing," reducing the slave to an article of property which no longer has a self. But selfhood, and the ability to refer to "my" and "mine," is an absolute and intrinsic right bestowed upon humans by God. To deprive a person of it is such an egregious offense that it undermines the entire moral order established by God.

The spirit of slavery never seeks shelter in the Bible, of its own accord. It grasps the horns of the altar only in desperation—rushing from the terror of the avenger's arm. Like other unclean spirits, it "hateth the light, neither cometh to the light, lest its deeds should be reproved" [John 3:20]. Goaded to frenzy in its conflicts with conscience and common sense, denied all quarter, and hunted from every covert, it vaults over the sacred enclosure and courses up and down the Bible, "seeking rest, and finding none" [Matthew

12:43]. The law of love, glowing on every page, flashes around it an omnipresent anguish and despair. It shrinks from the hated light, and howls under the consuming touch, as demons quailed before the Son of God, and shrieked, "Torment us not" [Luke 8:28]. At last, it slinks away under the types of the Mosaic system, and seeks to burrow out of sight among their shadows. Vain hope! Its asylum is its sepulcher; its city of refuge, the city of destruction. It flies from light into the sun; from heat, into devouring fire; and from the voice of God into the thickest of His thunders.

If we would know whether the Bible sanctions slavery, we must determine *what slavery is*. A constituent element, is one thing; a relation, another; an appendage, another. Relations and appendages presuppose *other* things to which they belong. To regard them as *the things themselves*, or as constituent parts of them, leads to endless fallacies. A great variety of conditions, relations, and tenures, indispensable to the social state, are confounded with slavery; and thus slaveholding becomes quite harmless, if not virtuous. We will specify some of those.

1. *Privation of suffrage*. Then minors are slaves.

2. *Ineligibility to office*. Then females are slaves.

3. *Taxation without representation*. Then slaveholders in the District of Columbia are slaves.

4. *Privation of one's oath in law*. Then disbelievers in a future retribution are slaves.

5. *Privation of trial by jury*. Then all in France and Germany are slaves.

6. *Being required to support a particular religion*. Then the people of England are slaves. (To the preceding may be added all other disabilities, merely *political*.)

7. *Cruelty and oppression.* Wives, children, and hired domestics are often oppressed; but these forms of cruelty are not slavery.

8. *Apprenticeship.* The rights and duties of master and apprentice are correlative and reciprocal. The *claim* of each upon the other results from his *obligation* to the other. Apprenticeship is based on the principle of equivalent for value received. The rights of the apprentice are secured, equally with those of the master. Indeed, while the law is *just* to the master, it is *benevolent* to the apprentice. Its main design is rather to benefit the apprentice than the master. It promotes the interests of the former, while in doing it, it guards from injury those of the latter. To the master it secures a mere legal compensation—to the apprentice, both a legal compensation and a virtual gratuity in addition, he being of the two the greatest gainer. The law not only recognizes the *right* of the apprentice to a reward for his labor, but appoints the wages, and enforces the payment. The master's claim covers only the *services* of the apprentice. The apprentice's claim covers *equally* the services of the master. Neither can hold the other as property; but each holds property in the services of the other, and both equally. Is this slavery?

9. *Filial subordination and parental claims.* Both are nature's dictates and intrinsic elements of the social state; the natural affections which blend parent and child in one, excite each to discharge those offices incidental to the relation, and constitute a shield for mutual protection. The parent's legal claim to the child's services, while a minor, is a slight return for the care and toil of his rearing, to say nothing of outlays for support and education. This provision is, with the mass of mankind, indispensable to the preservation of the family state. The child, in helping his parents, helps himself—increases a common stock, in which he has a share; while his most faithful services do but acknowledge a debt that money cannot cancel.

10. *Bondage for crime.* Must innocence be punished because guilt suffers penalties? True, the criminal works for the government

without pay; and well he may. He owes the government. A century's work would not pay its drafts on him. He is a public de-
faulter, and will die so. Because laws make men pay their debts,
shall those be forced to pay who owe nothing? The law makes no
criminal, property. It restrains his liberty, and makes him pay
something, a mere penny in the pound, of his debt to the government; but it does not make him a chattel. Test it. To own property, is to own its product. Are children born of convicts,
government property? Besides, can *property* be guilty? Are chattels punished?

11. *Restraints upon freedom.* Children are restrained by parents—
pupils, by teachers—patients, by physicians—corporations, by
charters—and legislatures, by constitutions. Embargoes, tariffs,
quarantine, and all other laws, keep men from doing as they
please. Restraints are the web of society, warp and woof. Are they
slavery? Then civilized society is a giant slave—a government
of law, *the climax of slavery*, and its executive, a king among slaveholders.

12. *Compulsory service.* A juryman is empaneled against his will, and
sit he must. A sheriff orders his posse; bystanders *must* turn in. Men
are *compelled* to remove nuisances, pay fines and taxes, support
their families, and "turn to the right as the law directs," however
much against their wills. Are they therefore slaves? To confound
slavery with involuntary service is absurd. Slavery is a *condition*.
The slave's *feelings* toward it, are one thing; the condition itself,
is another thing; his feelings cannot alter the nature of that condition. Whether he desires or detests it, the condition remains
the same. The slave's willingness to be a slave is no palliation of
the slaveholder's guilt. Suppose the slave should think himself a
chattel, and consent to be so regarded by others, does
that *make* him a chattel, or make those guiltless who *hold* him as
such? I may be sick of life, and I tell the assassin so that stabs me;
is he any the less a murderer? Does my *consent* to his crime, atone

for it? My partnership in his guilt, blot out his part of it? The slave's willingness to be a slave, so far from lessening the guilt of the "owner," aggravates it. If slavery has so palsied his mind that he looks upon himself as a chattel, and consents to be one, actually to hold him as such, falls in with his delusion, and confirms the impious falsehood. These very feelings and convictions of the slave, (if such were possible) increase a hundredfold the guilt of the master, and call upon him in thunder, immediately to recognize him as a man, and thus break the sorcery that cheats him out of his birthright—the consciousness of his worth and destiny.

Many of the foregoing conditions are *appendages* of slavery. But no one, nor all of them together, constitute its intrinsic unchanging element.

We proceed to state affirmatively that, enslaving men is reducing them to articles of property—making free agents, chattels —converting *persons*, into *things*—sinking immortality, into *merchandize*. A *slave* is one held in this condition. In law, "he owns nothing, and can acquire nothing."

His right to himself is abrogated. If he say my hands, my feet, my body, my mind, myself, they are figures of speech. To *use himself* for his own good, is a crime. To keep what he *earns*, is stealing. To take his body into his own keeping, is *insurrection*. In a word, the *profit* of his master is made the end of his being, and he, a *mere means* to that end—a *mere means* to an end into which his interests do not enter, of which they constitute no portion. Man, sunk to a *thing!* the intrinsic element, the *principle* of slavery; men, bartered, leased, mortgaged, bequeathed, invoiced, shipped in cargoes, stored as goods, taken on executions, and knocked off at public outcry! Their *rights*, another's conveniences; their interests, wares on sale; their happiness, a household utensil; their personal inalienable ownership, a serviceable article, or a plaything, as best suits the humor of the hour; their deathless nature, science, social affections, sympathies, hopes—

marketable commodities! We repeat it, *the reduction of persons to things*; not robbing a man of privileges, but of *himself*; not loading with burdens, but making him a *beast of burden*; not *restraining* liberty, but subverting it; not curtailing rights, but abolishing them; not inflicting personal cruelty, but annihilating *personality*; not exacting involuntary labor, but sinking him into an *implement* of labor; not abridging human comforts, but abrogating human nature; not depriving an animal of immunities, but despoiling a rational being of attributes—uncreating a man, to make room for a *thing!*

That this is American slavery, is shown by the laws of slave states. Judge Stroud,* in his "Sketch of the Laws relating to Slavery," says, "The cardinal principle of slavery, that the slave is not to be ranked among sentient beings, but among *things*—obtains as undoubted law in all of these [the slave] states." The law of South Carolina thus lays down the principle, "Slaves shall be deemed, held, taken, reputed, and adjudged in law to be chattels personal in the hands of their owners and possessors, and their executors, administrators, and assigns, to all intents, constructions, and purposes whatsoever."—Brevard's Digest, 229. In Louisiana, "A slave is one who is in the power of a master to whom he belongs; the master may sell him, dispose of his person, his industry, and his labor; he can do nothing, possess nothing, nor acquire anything, but what must belong to his master."—Civ. Code of Louisiana, Art. 35.

This is American slavery. The eternal distinction between a person and a thing, trampled underfoot—the crowning distinction of all others—alike the source, the test, and the measure of their value—the rational, immortal principle, consecrated by God to universal homage, in a baptism of glory and honor by the gift of His Son, His Spirit, His word, His presence, providence, and power; His shield, and staff, and sheltering wing; His opening

---

*George M. Stroud (1795–1875), American jurist.

heavens, and angels ministering, and chariots of fire, and songs of morning stars, and a great voice in heaven, proclaiming eternal sanctions, and confirming the word with signs following.

Having stated the *principle* of American slavery, we ask, Does the Bible sanction such a principle? "To the *law* and the *testimony?*" First, the moral law. Just after the Israelites were emancipated from their bondage in Egypt, while they stood before Sinai to receive the law, as the trumpet waxed louder, and the mount quaked and blazed, God spake the ten commandments from the midst of clouds and thunderings. *Two* of those commandments deal death to slavery. "Thou shalt not steal," [Exodus 20:15] or, "thou shalt not take from another what belongs to him." All man's powers are God's gift to *him*. That they are *his own*, is proved from the fact that God has given them to *him alone*,—that each of them is a part of himself, and all of them together constitute himself. All else that belongs to man, is acquired by the *use* of these powers. The interest belongs to him, because the principal does; the product is his, because he is the producer. Ownership of anything, is ownership of its *use*. The right to use according to will, is *itself* ownership. The eighth commandment presupposes and assumes the right of every man to his powers, and their product. Slavery robs of both. A man's right to himself, is the only right absolutely original and intrinsic—his right to whatever else that belongs to him is merely *relative* to this, is derived from it, and held only by virtue of it. Self-right is the *foundation right*—the *post in the middle*, to which all other rights are fastened. Slaveholders, when talking about their right to their slaves, always assume their own right to themselves. What slaveholder ever undertook to prove his right to himself? He knows it to be a self-evident proposition, that *a man belongs to himself*— that the right is intrinsic and absolute. In making out his own title, he makes out the title of every human being. As the fact of being *a man* is itself the title, the whole human family have one common title deed. If one man's title is valid, all are valid. If one is worthless, all are. To deny the validity of the *slave's* title is to deny the validity of *his own*; and yet in the act of making a man a slave, the slaveholder *asserts* the validity of his own title, while he seizes him as his property who has the *same* title. Further, in making him a slave, he does not merely disfranchise the humanity of *one* individual, but of universal man. He destroys the foundations. He annihilates *all rights*. He attacks not only the human race, but *universal being*, and rushes upon Jehovah. For rights are *rights*; God's are no more—man's are no less.

The eighth commandment forbids the taking of *any part* of that which belongs to another. Slavery takes the *whole*. Does the same Bible which prohibits the taking of *any*thing from him, sanction the taking of *every*thing? Does it thunder wrath against him who robs his neighbor of a *cent*, yet bid God speed to him who robs his neighbor of *himself*? Slaveholding is the highest possible violation of the eighth commandment. To take from a man his earnings, is theft. But to take the *earner*, is a compound, lifelong theft—supreme robbery, that vaults up the climax at a leap—the dread, terrific, giant robbery, that towers among other robberies a solitary horror, monarch of the realm. The eighth commandment forbids the taking away, and the *tenth* adds, "thou shalt not covet anything that is thy neighbor's" [Exodus 20:17]; thus guarding every man's right to himself and his property, by making not only the actual taking away a sin, but even that state of mind which would *tempt* to it. Whoever made human beings slaves, without *coveting* them? Why take from them their time, labor, liberty, right of self-preservation and improvement, their right to acquire property, to worship according to conscience, to search the Scriptures, to live with their families, and their right to their own bodies, if they do not *desire* them? They covet them for purposes of gain, convenience, lust of dominion, of sensual gratification, of pride and ostentation. They break the tenth commandment, and pluck down upon their heads the plagues that are written in the book.—*Ten* commandments constitute the brief compendium of human duty.—*Two* of these brand slavery as sin.

The giving of the law at Sinai, immediately preceded the promulgation of that body of laws called the "Mosaic system." Over the gateway of that system, fearful words were written by the finger of God—"He that stealeth a man and selleth him, or if he be found in his hand, he shall surely be put to death." Ex. xxi. 16.

SOURCE: Theodore Dwight Weld, *The Bible Against Slavery*, 3rd edition. (New York: Anti–American Slavery Society, 1838), 5-11.

I Am an Abolitionist (1841)

William Lloyd Garrison

The abolitionist movement gave rise to a great many hymns, often set to familiar tunes, that expressed hopes for an end to slavery. They were frequently sung at anti-slavery gatherings, and several compilations of them were published. Their purpose was not merely to inspire, but also to offer sentiments and slogans that would lodge in the memory.

William Lloyd Garrison's "I Am an Abolitionist" was one of the most popular. Sung to the tune of "Auld Lang Syne," it reminded abolitionists that their campaign against slavery was waged "in God's great name." Given the holiness of the crusade—"a nobler strife the world ne'er saw"—as well as faith in "God's great strength," the hymn urged slavery's foes not to be dismayed by danger and disappointment.

I am an Abolitionist!
I glory in the name:
Though now by Slavery's minions hiss'd
And covered o'er with shame,
It is a spell of light and power—
The watchword of the free:—
Who spurns it in the trial-hour,
A craven soul is he!

I am an Abolitionist!
Then urge me not to pause;
For joyfully do I enlist
In FREEDOM'S sacred cause:

A nobler strife the world ne'er saw,
Th' enslaved to disenthrall;
I am a soldier for the war,
Whatever may befall!

I am an Abolitionist!
Oppression's deadly foe;
In God's great strength will I resist,
And lay the monster low;
In God's great name do I demand,
To all be freedom given,
That peace and joy may fill the land,
And songs go up to heaven!

I am an Abolitionist!
No threats shall awe my soul,
No perils cause me to desist,
No bribes my nets control;
A freeman will I live and die,
In sunshine and in shade,
And raise my voice for liberty,
Of nought on earth afraid.

I am an Abolitionist—
The tyrant's hate and dread—
The friend of all who are oppressed—
A price is on my head!
My country is the wide, wide world,
My countrymen mankind:
Down to the dust be Slavery hurled!
All servile chains unbind!

Source: William Lloyd Garrison, "I Am an Abolitionist," in *The Anti-Slavery Harp*, ed. William W. Brown (Boston: Bela Marsh, 1848), 17–18.

Appeal to the Followers of Christ (1842)

Cassius M. Clay

A wealthy Kentucky planter who declared himself an abolitionist, freed his slaves, and then offered them jobs as wage laborers, Cassius Clay (1810–1903) was reviled by fellow southerners for what they saw as his betrayal of their way of life. But Clay, who served for a while in the Kentucky state house and, later, as U.S. ambassador to Russia, wanted nothing to do with what he called the "slavocracy." His outspoken opposition to human bondage brought at least three attacks on his life by furious proponents of slavery.

In this piece, Clay argues that slavery is not only a political and social blight upon the land but is also contrary to the will of God and the teachings of Christ. Slavery, he writes, is the "nation's great sin" and calls upon "every follower of Christ to bear testimony against this crime against man and God."

To all the adherents of the Christian religion, Catholic and Protestant, in the American Union, the writer of this article would respectfully represent, that he is but a single individual of humble pretensions struggling with honest zeal for the liberties of his country and the common rights of mankind. He sets up no claims to piety or purity of life; but whilst he is himself subject to all the infirmities of our common nature, he believes in an omnipotent and benevolent God over-ruling the universe by fixed and eternal laws. He believes that man's greatest happiness consists in a wise understanding and a strict observance of all the laws of his being, moral, mental, and physical; which are best set forth in the Christian code of ethics. He believes that the Christian religion is the truest basis of justice, mercy, truth, and happiness, known among men. As a politician especially, does he regard Christian morality as the basis of national and constitutional liberty. He believes, that liberty of conscience was the antecedent of civil liberty, and that to Christianity did our fathers owe the emigration from the Old World, and our national independence in the New. He believes that there is now a crisis in the affairs of our nation, which calls for the united efforts of all good men to save us from dishonor and ruin.

Slavery is our great national sin, and must be destroyed, or we are lost. From a small cloud, not larger than a man's hand, it has overspread the whole heavens. Three millions of our fellow men, all children of the same Father, are held in absolute servitude, and the most unqualified despotism. By a strange oversight, or self-avenging criminality of our fathers, an anti-republican, unequal, sham representation has given the slavocracy a concerted power which subjects the additional fifteen million of whites of this nation to the caprice and rule of some three hundred and fifty thousand slaveholders. They monopolize the principal offices of honor and profit, control our foreign relations, and internal policy of economical progress. They have forced us into unjust wards—national bad faith—and large and unnecessary expenditures of money. They have violated, time after time, the national and state Constitutions. They have trampled under foot all of the cardinal principles of our inherited liberty—freedom of the press—liberty of speech—trial by jury—the habeas corpus, and that clause of the constitution which gives to the citizens of the several states the rights and privileges of citizens of each state. They have murdered our citizens—imprisoned our seamen—and denied us all redress in the courts of national judicature, by forcibly and illegally expelling our ambassadors—thus failing in the comity, observed sacred by all nations, civilized, and savage, till now! All this we have borne, in magnanimous forbearance, or tame subservience; till remonstrance is regarded as criminal; and it has become the common law of the land, in all the states, to murder in cold blood, and in a calm and "dignified manner," any American freeman, who has the spirit to exercise the constitutional, and natural, and inalienable rights of free thought and manly utterance!

Now, in the name of that religion which teaches us to love our neighbor as ourself—to do unto others as we would have others should do unto us—to break every yoke, and let the oppressed go free—we pray every follower of Christ to bear testimony against this crime against man and God; which fills our souls with cruelty and crime—stains our hands with blood—and overthrows every principle of national and constitutional liberty, for which the good and great souled patriots of all ages laid down their lives, and for which our fathers suffered, bled, and died.

We pray you to set your faces against all those professed followers of Christ, who betray him in the house of his friends, and make God out the founder of an institution which causes the most refined, enlightened, and respectable men in the state of Kentucky, where slavery exists in its most modified and lenient supremacy, to raise the black and bloody flag of death to liberty of speech and the press!

We pray you in the name of liberty—our country—our common humanity—and the God of all, who is no respecter of persons—to come to our help!

SOURCE: *The Writings of Cassius Marcellus Clay: including speeches and addresses,* ed. Horace Greeley (New York: Harper & Brothers, 1848), 358–59.

An Address to the Slaves of the United States of America (1843)

Henry Highland Garnet

Born a slave, Henry Highland Garnet (1815–1882) escaped bondage with his entire family and was raised as a free man in New York City. Highly educated and deeply religious, he was ordained a Presbyterian minister and served congregations in New York, Pennsylvania, and Washington, DC.

Early in his career, Garnet briefly advocated for the migration of freed slaves, arguing that nearly any other country besides the United States offered them a friendlier home. But he eventually rejected this idea and turned his attention instead to the self-emancipation of slaves. Claiming that both their bondage and passive acquiescence to it were sins in God's eyes, Garnet argued, as in this speech delivered to the National Convention of Colored Persons, that slaves had a religious obligation to resist and even rebel against their captivity. Garnet's call to arms was rejected by many of his fellow Christian abolitionists. But it anticipated John Brown's 1859 raid on Harpers Ferry intended to provoke an armed slave rebellion.

Two hundred and twenty-seven years ago, the first of our injured race were brought to the shores of America. They came not with glad spirits to select their homes in the New World. They came not with their own consent, to find an unmolested enjoyment of the blessings of this fruitful soil. The first dealings they had with men calling themselves Christians, exhibited to them the worst features of corrupt and sordid hearts: and convinced them that no cruelty is too great, no villainy and no robbery too abhorrent for even enlightened men to perform, when influenced by avarice and lust. Neither did they come flying upon the wings of Liberty, to a land of freedom. But they came with broken hearts, from their beloved native land, and were doomed to unrequited toil and deep degradation. Nor did the evil of their bondage end at their emancipation by death. Succeeding generations inherited their chains, and millions have come from eternity into time, and have returned again to the world of spirits, cursed and ruined by American slavery.

The propagators of the system, or their immediate ancestors, very soon discovered its growing evil, and its tremendous wickedness, and secret promises were made to destroy it. The gross inconsistency of a people holding slaves, who had themselves "ferried o'er the wave" for freedom's sake, was too apparent to be entirely overlooked. The voice of Freedom cried, "Emancipate your slaves." Humanity supplicated with tears for the deliverance of the children of Africa. Wisdom urged her solemn plea. The bleeding captive pleaded his innocence, and pointed to Christianity who stood weeping at the cross. Jehovah frowned upon the nefarious institution, and thunderbolts, red with vengeance, struggled to leap forth to blast the guilty wretches who maintained it. But all was vain. Slavery had stretched its dark wings of death over the land, the Church stood silently by—the priests prophesied falsely, and the people loved to have it so. Its throne is established, and now it reigns triumphant.

Nearly three millions of your fellow-citizens are prohibited by law and public opinion (which in this country is stronger than law) from reading the Book of Life. Your intellect has been destroyed as much as possible, and every ray of light they have attempted to shut out from your minds. The oppressors themselves have become involved in the ruin. They have become weak, sensual, and rapacious—they have cursed you—they have cursed themselves—they have cursed the earth which they have trod.

Slavery! How much misery is comprehended in that single word. What mind is there that does not shrink from its direful effects? Unless the image of God be obliterated from the soul, all men cherish the love of Liberty. The nice discerning political economist does not regard the sacred right more than the untutored African who roams in the wilds of Congo. Nor has the one more right to the full enjoyment of his freedom than the other. In every man's mind the good seeds of liberty are planted, and he who brings his fellow down so low, as to make him contented with a condition of slavery, commits the highest crime against God and man. Brethren, your oppressors aim to do this. They endeavor to make you as much like brutes as possible....

To such Degradation it is sinful in the Extreme for you to make voluntary Submission. The divine commandments you are in duty bound to reverence and obey. If you do not obey them, you will surely meet with the displeasure of the Almighty. He requires you to love him supremely, and your neighbor as yourself—to keep the Sabbath day holy—to search the Scriptures—and bring up your children with respect for his laws, and to worship no other God but him. But slavery sets all these at naught, and hurls defiance in the face of Jehovah. The forlorn condition in which you are placed, does not destroy your moral obligation to God. You are not certain of heaven, because you suffer yourselves to remain in a state of slavery, where you cannot obey the commandments of the Sovereign of the universe. If the ignorance of slavery is a passport to heaven, then it is a blessing, and no curse, and you should rather desire its perpetuity than its abolition. God will not receive slavery, nor ignorance, nor any other state of mind, for love and obedience to him. Your condition does not absolve you from your moral obligation. The diabolical injustice by which your liberties are cloven down, NEITHER GOD NOR ANGELS, OR JUST MEN, COMMAND YOU TO SUFFER FOR A SINGLE MOMENT. THEREFORE IT IS YOUR SOLEMN AND IMPERATIVE DUTY TO USE EVERY

MEANS, BOTH MORAL, INTELLECTUAL AND PHYSI-
CAL THAT PROMISES SUCCESS. If a band of heathen men
should attempt to enslave a race of Christians, and to place their
children under the influence of some false religion, surely,
Heaven would frown upon the men who would not resist such ag-
gression, even to death. If, on the other hand, a band of Christians should attempt to enslave a race of heathen men, and to
entail slavery upon them, and to keep them in heathenism in the
midst of Christianity, the God of heaven would smile upon every
effort which the injured might make to disenthrall themselves...

We do not advise you to attempt a revolution with the sword,
because it would be inexpedient. Your numbers are too small, and
moreover the rising spirit of the age, and the spirit of the gospel,
are opposed to war and bloodshed. But from this moment cease
to labor for tyrants who will not remunerate you. Let every slave
throughout the land do this, and the days of slavery are num-
bered. You cannot be more oppressed than you have been—you
cannot suffer greater cruelties than you have already. Rather die
freemen, than live to be slaves. Remember that you are THREE
MILLIONS.

It is in your power so to torment the God-cursed slaveholders, that they will be glad to let you go free. If the scale was
turned, and black men were the masters and white men the
slaves, every destructive agent and element would be employed
to lay the oppressor low. Danger and death would hang over their
heads day and night. Yes, the tyrants would meet with plagues
more terrible than those of Pharaoh. But you are a patient people.
You act as though you were made for the special use of these devils. You act as though your daughters were born to pamper the
lusts of your masters and overseers. And worse than all, you
tamely submit while your lords tear your wives from your em-
braces and defile them before your eyes. In the name of God, we
ask, are you men? Where is the blood of your fathers? Has it all

run out of your veins? Awake, awake; millions of voices are calling you! Your dead fathers speak to you from their graves. Heaven, as with a voice of thunder, calls on you to arise from the dust.

Let your motto be resistance! Resistance! Resistance! No oppressed people have ever secured their liberty without resistance. What kind of resistance you had better make, you must decide by the circumstances that surround you, and according to the suggestion of expediency. Brethren, adieu! Trust in the living God. Labor for the peace of the human race, and remember that you are three millions.

Source: *Walker's Appeal, with a Brief Sketch of His Life by Henry Highland Garnet. And Also Garnet's Address to the Slaves of the United States of America* (New York: J. H. Tobitt, 1848), 90–93, 96–97.

I Am Pleading for My People (1840s)

Sojourner Truth

Born Isabella Baumfree, Sojourner Truth (1797–1883) escaped from slavery when she was thirty years old. She had managed to take an infant daughter with her. One year later, she successfully sued in a court of law for the freedom of a son she'd been forced to leave behind. She renamed herself in 1843 after receiving a call from God to preach truth throughout the land.

In the years leading up to the Civil War, Sojourner Truth spoke tirelessly at abolitionist meetings across the country. She also became a supporter of women's rights, delivering a now famous speech, "Ain't I a Woman?" at the 1851 Women's Rights Convention in Akron, Ohio.

Truth never learned to read or write, and her speeches were always extemporaneous. Sometimes, to get her point across, she would break out in songs composed on the spot. "I Am Pleading for My People," sung to the tune of "Auld Lang Syne," is one of her most moving ones. In it, she pulls no punches in describing the horrors of slavery. But she refuses to hate or seek vengeance upon slave owners. Instead, she appeals to conscience.

I am pleading for my people, a poor downtrodden race
Who dwell in freedom's boasted land with no abiding place.
I am pleading that my people may have their rights restored,
for they have long been toiling, and yet had no reward.

They are forced the crops to culture, but not for them they yield,
Although both late and early, they labor in the field.

While I bear upon my body, the scores of many a gash,
I'm pleading for my people who groan beneath the lash.

I'm pleading for the mothers who gaze in wild despair
Upon the hated auction block, and see their children there.
I feel for those in bondage—well may I feel for them.
I know how fiendish hearts can be that sell their fellow men.

Yet those oppressors steeped in guilt—I still would have them
    live;
For I have learned of Jesus, to suffer and forgive!
I want no carnal weapons, no machinery of death.
For I love to not hear the sound of war's tempestuous breath.

I do not ask you to engage in death and bloody strife.
I do not dare insult my God by asking for their life.
But while your kindest sympathies to foreign lands do roam,
I ask you to remember your own oppressed at home.

I plead with you to sympathize with signs and groans and scars,
And note how base the tyranny beneath the stripes and stars.

SOURCE: *Narrative of Sojourner Truth*, ed. Olive Gilbert (Battle
Creek, MI: Review and Herald Office, 1884), 302–4.

A Condensed Anti-Slavery
Biblical Argument (1845)

George Bourne

English-born George Bourne (1780–1845), who immigrated to the United States in 1804, was a Dutch Reformed minister who was one of the most outspoken pulpit opponents of slavery, even expelling slave owners from his congregations. He is credited with being the first American abolitionist to call for immediate rather than gradual emancipation.

In this selection, Bourne argues that slavery not only violates the moral principle that each person has an equal right to freedom but also breaks each one of the Ten Commandments. How then, he asks, can human bondage possibly be the will of God?

At the creation God gave to mankind alone, the dominion of ownership or property in the earth and its productions. By virtue of this great statutory grant, one individual of the human race has just as good natural and divine right to the earth and its productions as any other individual has, of which right every kind of monopoly is a direct infringement and breach of the oral law of God, and to the full and perfect enjoyment of which grant and right, it is necessary that each individual should be just as free as all the rest are. This statute strikes at the root of not only slavery, but of monopoly; by rendering such a violation of the moral law. Thus does the first chapter in the Scriptures contain, by an implied but necessary divine guarantee, the grand charter of the civil liberties of all mankind—a charter violated by slaveholders, and other monopolists, and by oppressors every moment of their oppressive agency. God himself has thus forbidden all human monopoly by His own holy and perfect law. He never made a grant to one class of men of any other class, and the fact that he has not is alone proof certain and conclusive that so far from ever having sanctioned the practice of human slavery, He utterly forbade the same by enactments, obedience to which rendered such slavery impossible.

Another equally decisive fact is that human slavery is a direct violation of the eighth and tenth commandments, and an indirect but equally certain violation of the other commands contained in that great table. Slavery is the highest kind of larceny, and is therefore the greatest possible violation of the eighth commandment. But as by the same law every human being is, under God, the sole owner of himself and all his just rights, faculties and acquisitions, the crime which usurps and robs him of them all is founded in covetousness, or in a greedy and criminal desire to possess that which belongs to another, or to others, and to which the slaveholder knows he has no moral or just right, and which is thus a direct violation of the tenth commandment.

But human slavery is also an indirect but equally certain violation of the commands in the Decalogue because its support and effects necessarily produce such violations as every reader will by a little reflection readily perceive. Now nothing could be more wickedly absurd than the supposition, that though the Almighty enacted these great commands, He at the same time established an institution in the same law, the support of which he knew would produce the necessary and certain violation of the same commands, and within the wide sphere of its destructive influence, render the practical observance and operation of the whole of them impossible.

Slavery produces the constant violation of the commands of the Decalogue. Thus, it compels the slaves to violate the first and second commands, by rendering their masters the objects of their slavish obedience and worship, and compelling them to obey their owners' will in every case, though that will be ever so hostile to that of God. It produces the violation of the third command, by the constant criminal temptation and wicked necessity in all concerned in, or suffering from it, to use the most profane language, and causes them otherwise lightly to treat their Maker's commands. It reaches them also to violate the fourth command. By rendering it impossible for slaves to observe the Lord's day (the Christian's Sabbath), in the spirit of the command, and by otherwise inducing a general neglect and disregard in all slave societies to the ordinances to be attended to on that day; of the fifth, by prohibiting slave children from honoring and obeying their own parents, they being obliged to substitute in place of filial obedience and parental authority, a slavish obedience and subjection to their masters only; of the sixth, by constantly tempting and producing slave murders in every form and degree of barbarity, for the necessary support of slavery; of the seventh, by prohibiting marriage to the slaves, and producing criminal concubinage and licentiousness among them, as well as the general compulsory prostitution of the female portion of the slaves, by reason of the arbitrary power which it confers on the masters and other oppressors; and lastly, of the ninth, by its necessary tendency to produce the habit of falsehood and lying in both masters and slaves—in the former for the purpose of deceiving and abusing their slaves, in the latter to deceive their oppressors and avoid punishment for slave offences.

It also produces the same habit in others who are infected with the spirit of the sin of slavery and are enlisted in its support, as is well exemplified by their constant employment of the various false pretenses and objections raised by them against the abolition of slavery, and by the malignant falsehoods circulated by them against the friends of emancipation, and their measures, as well as against and respecting slaves; and as all the other moral precepts in the Scriptures are but exemplifications and applications of those in the Decalogue, slavery directly or indirectly produces the constant necessary violation of them all.

The last decisive fact I shall quote in this connection is that human slavery is an indirect but certain violation of every moral precept contained in the Scriptures because the support of it produces the necessary violation of every one of those precepts, a circumstance which proves its great criminality. In this way such slavery is discovered to violate the spirit or general intent of the Scriptures more extensively perhaps than any other crime except murder. It is impossible for any person to practice human slavery an hour without violating the law of Love, the Golden Rule, and the numerous other similar precepts that abound in the Scriptures, as much so as if he practiced murder and other crimes, as everyone would acknowledge were he himself enslaved, and as the slightest critical reflection will demonstrate.

SOURCE: A Citizen of Virginia (George Bourne), *A Condensed Anti-Slavery Bible Argument* (New York: S. W. Benedict, 1845), 62–65.

The Sinfulness of Slaveholding (1846)

James G. Birney

Born into a Kentucky slaveholding family, James Birney (1792–1857) eventually became a proponent of immediate emancipation and ran twice for the presidency as the candidate of the anti-slavery Liberty Party. His turnabout on the topic of slavery seems to have been the consequence of a religious conversion experience.

In this selection, he argues that slavery is a "positive" act of coercive force on the part of one person to dominate another. Such an act is unlawful, if for no other reason than that it violates the Golden Rule and hence is contrary to God's will. Birney offers a parable about an African prince who kidnaps members of a neighboring village and sells them to a slave trader who in turn sells them to a South Carolina planter. The prince may have no notion of the Golden Rule and the trader only a dim one. But the planter, a proper churchgoer, knows it full well. Consequently, even though all three men have sinned, the planter is guiltier than the first two. In offering this parable, Birney clearly suggests that slavery-supporting clergy, learned in scripture, are the guiltiest of all.

To the Preachers of the Gospel in the United States

Gentlemen—

This is dedicated to you, inasmuch as it is written chiefly for you. It is intended, for the most part, for intelligent and well-trained minds; therefore, it is but the suggestion of thoughts which lie still more expanded in the mind of the writer.

The writer does not believe that slavery can be established by any law. It is out of the power of man, as adultery, murder, profanity would be. No human law that requires me to speak irreverently of the Author of my existence, or to commit any of the crimes mentioned in the Decalogue, is of any binding obligation. Slavery has been *might*, prevailing for a season against *right*. The strong and unprincipled have enslaved the weak and defenseless, till it has emasculated the former. As slavery is now a sign of weakness in the nation that cherishes it, so is it a sign of weakness in the tribes that permit it.

I will not withhold my surprise, that any of you should still use the Book of God's *love* to countenance the practice of Man's *hate*. HE has formed me, in some sort, to see HIM as a God of love, as a God of justice—as a Father, tender and kind; as a Governor, just and inflexible. He has bestowed on me the faculties of *love* and *justice*. They must be like his own. I must, therefore, throw aside his character, and the book which reveals it, or I must throw aside its opposite, American Slavery, "the sum of villanies." To maintain them both is impossible. Which of them I shall throw aside, I leave to you. . . .

The question to be determined is, Is Slaveholding right in any circumstances? I shall approach the subject without prejudice, and do what I can to lead all concerned to a right decision.

Let us first determine what slaveholding is; for why should we dispute about words, ignorant of what each other intends? Slaveholding is a positive act. I say this in opposition to a negative act. It is the absolute subjection of one human being to the will of another. It is not the voluntary going-out of the will of another, seeking a master, to whom he may, forever, thereafter, be irrevocably and totally surrendered; but the subduing of the will of another. This shows that something is to be done. The more his will be subdued to act on the instigation of another, the better slave he will make. Slaveholding, is, therefore, not a negative, but a positive act—a bringing under another's dominion, by force.

I say, by force: for it requires some application of force to subdue the will of another to conform in any degree to that of mine. If there was no slaveholding, there would be no slaveholder: if there was no slaveholder, there would be no subduing of the will by force. This force is unlawful, too, because it is exerted contrary to the will of him who is to be enslaved, and who has a right to be consulted. It, therefore, appears to be an act of unlawful force.

Jesus Christ, when he said, "whatever ye would that men should do to you, do ye even so to them" [Matthew 7:12], spoke to his hearers no revelation. It was what their reason would require of them; for just so far as they respected the rights of others, their rights would be respected—no further. And, to this day, this constitutes a good man. How far this influences savages, to whom the gospel has never been preached, we may learn from Dymond.* It is not pretended that this feeling exists, in the same degree, in the unrefined savage, as in the well-informed Christian; but that it does exist in all men sufficiently strong enough to be termed a law of our nature—one to be reasoned from.

If I am right in this—if it be true that slavery is attended with force; that this force is unlawful; that to do to others as they should do unto us, is the law that is common to human nature everywhere;—that to respect the rights of others, is the only security for having our own respected;—then, have I, already, to all impartial minds, fully made out my case. If these things be true, slavery cannot be right in its inception. And not being right in its inception, its subsequent continuance can never be right. A wrong, originating in a trespass, itself constituting a trespass, can never become a right. A plea to an assault and battery, that my

---

*Jonathan Dymond, *Essays on the Principles of Morals; and on the private and political rights and obligations of mankind* (New York: Collins, 1845), pp. 72–73.

intention was only to carry the party complaining into slavery, would, before a court and jury, uncontaminated with that system, avail me but little.

But as it is not impartial minds only, that are to be convinced, I will prosecute the inquiry a little further.

Admah is a savage African chief—He has about him and under his control, one hundred warriors. He is running short of rum, tobacco and balls. How shall he replenish his store! At that moment, a Christian slave-trader arrives on the coast, we will suppose, from Charleston, South Carolina. He is well supplied with the stores which Admah so much needs. He instigates him to adopt the most summary method of supplying his wants; to attack the village of his neighbor, Bolun, in the dead of the night, when the inmates are asleep and unsuspecting, and reduce as many of them as he can to slavery. Admah follows his advice. He attacks his neighbor, Bolun. Some fly in the dark; others resist by the light of their burning dwellings. The decrepit and immature he kills. When the struggle is over, he finds himself possessed of fifty strong men and women as slaves.

If, in the morning, his heart should relent, if he should say, I will not bind you, I will repair, as far as I can, the injury I have done, and you need not fear actual or constructive violence being hereafter applied to you, his victims would no longer be such, but they would at once go free. But Admah does not so act. He applies chains and fetters to their arms and limbs, and makes his captives his slaves.

Is Admah not here guilty of force? Is it not unlawful? Admah has attacked them in the dead of the night; they were his neighbors; and they depended on his friendship for Bolun, as a sufficient safeguard. Admah, in the best way he can, contrives to make them unsuspicious of his intended assault. Their not suspecting his friendship, makes his assault on them the surer. In this there was force. His secret preparations prove them to be unlawful, and his demeanor throughout the whole transaction, is a violation of the rule, written in his heart—"thou shalt do to others as you would that others should do unto you." It is plain, here, that he would not change conditions with his captives.

But Admah is not one of the pliant kind. He whips out of his captives their sulkiness—drives them, bound, to the sea-shore, and disposes of them for rum, tobacco and balls, to the international slave-trader. The slave-trader purchases—what? Not the bodies alone of the captives, because he has no use for them, and they are only an expense and encumbrance to him. He buys, beside, the power of the prince. The prince retires, with his warriors, from the position of force, and the slave-trader assumes it, with the necessary band. The situation of the captives remains unchanged. He applies as much of actual force, if it be necessary, as compels them to ascend the sides of his vessel, and as much of constructive force as keeps them conformed to his will.

In fine, he applies, just what Admah did, though in a different form—at least a competent degree of force for his object, which is keeping the captives in subjection to him. That it is a system of force—unlawful, of course, and prosecuted with an entire forgetfulness of the golden rule—may be easily tested. For, if the slave-trader were to tell them, at this time, that they might go about their business; that they might no longer fear actual or constructive force from him, or from any other quarter, they would at once go free.

In this way they are conveyed across the Atlantic, to the city of Charleston.

In the morning, one of the most intelligent planters visits the ship, desiring to purchase the whole lot, that he may add them to his stock. He confers with the slaveholder, and comes to an immediate agreement with him as to price. Actual force—the manacle—does not suit him. It does not consist with the business which he has for the captives to do. After a certain manner, he sets them at large, but he has, at the same time, impressed upon them, that if they claim the first right, to which, as men and equals, they are entitled to from him, there will be united against them, for the infliction of actual force, or death, it may be, all the whites, all the intelligence, and all the arms of the neighborhood; and, if it be necessary, of other States, and the General Government itself. He steps into the shoes of the slave-trader, as the slave-trader has before stepped into the shoes of the African prince.

So it is, with the descendants of the slaveholders, or of the purchasers from them in any succession.

What, then, is the difference of guilt between these three characters—the African prince, the slave-trader, and the planter? They occupy precisely the same position with regard to the captives. There is none—except it be this: the African prince is unlettered; in his mind, the rule by which we give to men all that we demand of them, may be comparatively faint; the slave-trader may have been brought up under the influences of Christianity, and this rule may be more clearly impressed upon him; whilst the planter may be a member of a Christian church, and the rule perfectly familiar to him. If we measure guilt by intelligence, we must suppose the planter the most guilty of the three. They all have exactly the same object, which is accomplished in the last....

I deem it anything but wise for the accredited ministers of God, to wrest the book of His *love*, which he has given to mankind for their happiness, to the maintenance of a system of *hate*, which greatly adds to their unhappiness. And I esteem it beyond historical dispute, that no people, who are greatly civilized, have ever admitted the system of slavery among them; and that it is a proof of advancing civilization, in any people, that they are getting rid of it. The present, then, I cannot but regard, at least, as an attempt on the part of the slave states, to impose a hindrance on the free states, to a further progress in true refinement and Christian civilization, for which they pant. If, knowing God's character as a God whose other name is *love*, some of his ministers in a slight degree had to *force* the book in which slavery was revealed, for its condemnation, it would not have been surprising; but, as a departure from slavery involved a national change, and a purification of their religion; as it would tend to throw into confusion everything that was done on that basis, and endanger the salaries and situation, for the time being, of themselves and their families, it is not unexpected that many have shown themselves unprepared for it. Be it understood, that I consider preachers of the gospel *as men;* that, as a class, they have the passions of men. I do not blame them because they do not act as angels. My heart has often bled for them, when I have seen the strait in which they were placed. So much I have thought it proper to say concerning the ministers of religion.

SOURCE: James G. Birney, *The Sinfulness of Slaveholding in All Circumstances; Tested by Reason and Scripture* (Detroit: Charles Willcox, 1846), iii, 5–8, 14.

The Anti-Slavery Alphabet (1846)

Hannah and Mary Townsend

Quaker sisters Hannah (1812–?) and Mary (1814–?) Townsend wrote and illustrated a sixteen-page chapbook to teach children the religious and moral evils of slavery. It was written expressly for an 1846 fundraising fair sponsored by the Philadelphia Female Anti-Slavery Society, a branch of the American Anti-Slavery Society. Touted by William Lloyd Garrison in the Liberator, the Townsend sisters' pamphlet became wildly popular.

"In the morning sow thy seed."

TO OUR LITTLE READERS.

Listen, little children, all,
Listen to our earnest call:
You are very young, 'tis true,
But there's much that you can do.
Even you can plead with men
That they buy not slaves again,
And that those they have may be
Quickly set at liberty.
They may hearken what *you* say,
Though from *us* they turn away.
Sometimes, when from school you walk,
You can with your playmates talk,

Tell them of the slave child's fate,
Motherless and desolate.
And you can refuse to take
Candy, sweetmeat, pie or cake,
Saying "no"—unless 'tis free—
"The slave shall not work for me."
Thus, dear little children, each
May some useful lesson teach;
Thus each one may help to free
This fair land from slavery.

A is an Abolitionist—
A man who wants to free
The wretched slave—and give to all
An equal liberty.

B is a Brother with a skin
Of somewhat darker hue,
But in our Heavenly Father's sight,
He is as dear as you.

C is the Cotton-field, to which
This injured brother's driven,
When, as the white-man's slave, he toils,
From early morn till even.

D is the Driver, cold and stern,
Who follows, whip in hand,
To punish those who dare to rest,
Or disobey command.

E is the Eagle, soaring high;
An emblem of the free;
But while we chain our brother man,
Our type he cannot be.

F is the heart-sick Fugitive,
The slave who runs away,
And travels through the dreary night,
But hides himself by day.

G is the Gong, whose rolling sound,
Before the morning light,
Calls up the little sleeping slave,
To labor until night.

H is the Hound his master trained,
And called to scent the track
Of the unhappy Fugitive,
And bring him trembling back.

I is the Infant, from the arms
Of its fond mother torn,
And, at a public auction, sold
With horses, cows, and corn.

J is the Jail, upon whose floor
That wretched mother lay,
Until her cruel master came,
And carried her away.

K is the Kidnapper, who stole
That little child and mother—
Shrieking, it clung around her, but
He tore them from each other.

L is the Lash, that brutally
He swung around its head,
Threatening that "if it cried again,
He'd whip it till 'twas dead."

M is the Merchant of the north,
Who buys what slaves produce—
So they are stolen, whipped and worked,
For his, and for our use.

N is the Negro, rambling free
In his far distant home,
Delighting 'neath the palm trees' shade
And cocoa-nut to roam.

O is the Orange tree, that bloomed
Beside his cabin door,
When white men stole him from his home
To see it never more.

P is the Parent, sorrowing,
And weeping all alone—
The child he loved to lean upon,
His only son, is gone!

Q is the Quarter, where the slave
On coarsest food is fed,
And where, with toil and sorrow worn,
He seeks his wretched bed.

R is the "Rice-swamp, dank and lone,"
Where, weary, day by day,
He labors till the fever wastes
His strength and life away.

S is the Sugar, that the slave
Is toiling hard to make,
To put into your pie and tea,
Your candy, and your cake.

T is the rank Tobacco plant,
Raised by slave labor too:
A poisonous and nasty thing,
For gentlemen to chew.

U is for Upper Canada,
Where the poor slave has found
Rest after all his wanderings,
For it is British ground!

V is the Vessel, in whose dark,
Noisome, and stifling hold,
Hundreds of Africans are packed,
Brought o'er the seas, and sold.

W is the Whipping post,
To which the slave is bound,
While on his naked back, the lash
Makes many a bleeding wound.

X is for Xerxes, famed of yore;
A warrior stern was he
He fought with swords; let truth and love
Our only weapons be.

Y is for Youth—the time for all
Bravely to war with sin;
And think not it can ever be
Too early to begin.

Z is a Zealous man, sincere,
Faithful, and just, and true;
An earnest pleader for the slave—
Will you not be so too?

Source: *The Anti-Slavery Alphabet* (Philadelphia: Merrihew & Thompson, 1847).

LECTURE TO
THE FEMALE ANTI-SLAVERY SOCIETY OF SALEM
(1847)

WILLIAM WELLS BROWN

Although not as well remembered today as his contemporary Frederick Douglass, Brown (1814–1884) had a remarkable career as an abolitionist and man of letters. Born into slavery in Kentucky, he escaped to Ohio as a young man and proceeded to write essays, a bestselling memoir, a novel loosely based on Thomas Jefferson's affair with Sally Hemings, and plays. He was also a dynamic public speaker.

In this selection from one of his orations, Brown insists that a slave is nothing more than a "piece of property" which may be disposed of in any way a white master sees fit. Reducing humans to the status of objects as it does, slavery "murders the soul." Brown especially singles out Christian clergy and associations, such as the American Bible Society and American Tract Society, for their cooperation, implicit or explicit, in slavery's "obliteration of the mind, crushing of the intellect, and annihilation of the soul."

What is a slave? A Slave is one that is in the power of an owner. He is a chattel; he is a thing; he is a piece of property. A master can dispose of him, can dispose of his labor, can dispose of his wife, can dispose of his offspring, can dispose of everything that belongs to the Slave, and the Slave shall have no right to speak; he shall have nothing to say. The Slave cannot speak for himself; he cannot speak for his wife, or his children. He is a thing. He is a piece of property in the hands of a master, as much as is the horse that belongs to the individual that may ride him through your streets tomorrow. Where we find one man holding an unlimited power over another, I ask, what can we expect to find his condition? Give one man power *ad infinitum* over another, and he will abuse that power; no matter if there be law; no matter if there be public sentiment in favor of the oppressed.

The system of Slavery, that I, in part, represent here this evening, is a system that strikes at the foundation of society, that strikes at the foundation of civil and political institutions. It is a system that takes man down from that lofty position which his God designed that he should occupy; that drags him down, places him upon a level with the beasts of the field, and there keeps him, that it may rob him of his liberty. Slavery is a system that tears the husband from the wife, and the wife from the husband; that tears the child from the mother, and the sister from the brother; that tears asunder the tenderest ties of nature. Slavery is a system that has its blood hounds, its chains, its negro whips, its dungeons, and almost every instrument of cruelty that the human eye can look at; and all this for the purpose of keeping the Slave in subjection; all this for the purpose of obliterating the mind, of crushing the intellect, and of annihilating the soul.

I have read somewhere of an individual named Caspar Hauser, who made his appearance in Germany some time since, and represented that he had made his escape from certain persons who had been trying to obliterate his mind, and to annihilate his intellect. The representation of that single individual raised such an excitement in Germany, that lawmakers took it in hand, examined it, and made a law covering that particular case and all cases that should occur of that kind; and they denominated it the "murder of the soul."* Now, I ask, what is Slavery doing in one

---

*Kaspar Hauser (1812?–1833) claimed to have escaped from a dark, small cellar when he was found wandering the streets of Nuremberg in 1828.

half of the States of this Union, at the present time? The souls of three millions of American citizens are being murdered every day under the blighting influence of American Slavery....

I ask, is not this a system that we should examine? Ought we not to look at it? Ought we not to see what the cause is that keeps the people asleep upon the great subject of American Slavery? When I get to talking about Slavery as it is, when I think of the three millions that are in chains at the present time, I am carried back to the days when I was a Slave upon a Southern plantation; I am carried back to the time when I saw dear relatives, with whom I am identified by the tenderest ties of nature, abused and ill-treated. I am carried back to the time when I saw hundreds of Slaves driven from the Slave-growing to the Slave-consuming States; when I begin to talk of Slavery, the sighs and the groans of three millions of my countrymen come to me upon the wings of every wind; and it causes me to feel sad, even when I think I am making a successful effort in representing the condition of the Slave....

I will therefore pass to the influence of Slavery upon the morals of the people; not only upon the morals of the Slavehold-ing South, or of the Slave, but upon the morals of the people of the United States of America. I am not willing to draw a line be-tween the people of the North and the people of the South. So far as the people of the North are connected with Slaveholding, they necessarily become contaminated by the evils that follow in the train of Slavery....

Talk about the influence of Slavery upon the morals of the people, when the Slave is sold in the Slaveholding States for the benefit of the church? When he is sold for the purpose of building churches? When he is sold for the benefit of the minister?...

Rumors about his parentage abounded, including the possibility that he was an illegitimate son of a member of the House of Baden. The jurist Anselm von Feuerbach (1775–1833), who wrote a book about Hauser and reformed the Bavarian legal system, coined the phrase "murder of the soul."

I have an advertisement, taken from a Charleston paper, advertising the property of a deceased Doctor of Divinity, probably one of the most popular men of his denomination that ever resided in the United States of America. In that advertisement it says, that among the property are "twenty-seven Negroes, two mules, one horse, and an old wagon." That is the property of a Slaveholding Doctor of Divinity!*

I have another advertisement before me, taken from an Alabama paper, in which eight Slaves are advertised to be sold for the benefit of an Old School Theological Seminary for the purpose of making ministers. I have another, where ten Slaves are advertised to be sold for the benefit of Christ Church Parish. I have another, where four Slaves are advertised to be sold for the benefit of the Missionary cause—a very benevolent cause indeed. I might go on and present to you advertisement after advertisement representing the system of American Slavery, and its contaminating influence upon the morals of the people. I have an account, very recent, that a Slave trader—one of the meanest and most degrading positions in which a man can be found upon God's footstool—buying and selling the bodies and souls of his fellow countrymen, has joined the church, and was, probably, hopefully converted. It is only an evidence that when Wickedness, with a purse of gold, knocks at the door of the Church, she seldom, if ever, is refused admission. . . .

Speak of the blighting influence of Slavery upon the morals of the people? Go into the Slaveholding States, and there you can see the master going into the church, on the Sabbath, with his Slave following him into the church, and waiting upon him—both belonging to the same church. And the day following, the master puts his slave upon the auction stand, and sells him to the highest bidder. The Church does not condemn him; the law does

---

*In a footnote, Brown identifies the Doctor of Divinity as Richard Furman (1755–1825), for whom South Carolina's Furman University is named.

not condemn him; public sentiment does not condemn him; but the Slaveholder walks through the community as much respected after he has sold a brother belonging to the same church with himself, as if he had not committed an offence against God.

Go into the Slaveholding States, and tomorrow you may see families of slaves driven to the auction stand, to be sold to the highest bidder; the husband to be sold in presence of the wife, the wife in presence of the husband, and the children in presence of them both. All this is done under the sanction of law and order; all is done under the sanction of public sentiment, whether that public sentiment be found in Church or in State.

Leaving the Slaveholding States, let me ask what is the influence that Slavery has over the minds of the Northern people? What is its contaminating influence over the great mass of the people of the North? It must have an influence, either good or bad. People of the North, being connected with the Slaveholding States, must necessarily become contaminated. Look all around, and you see benevolent associations formed for the purpose of carrying out the principles of Christianity; but what have they been doing for Humanity? What have they ever done for the Slave?

First, we see the great American Bible Society. It is sending bibles all over the world for the purpose of converting the heathen. Its agents are to be found in almost every country and climate. Yet three millions of Slaves have never received a single bible from the American Bible Society. A few years since, the American Anti-Slavery Society offered to the American Bible Society a donation of $5,000 if they would send bibles to the Slaves, or make an effort to do it, and the American Bible Society refused even to *attempt* to send the bible to the Slaves!

A Bible Society, auxiliary to the American Bible Society, held a meeting a short time since, at Cincinnati, in the State of Ohio. One of its members brought forward a resolution that the Society should do its best to put the bible into the hands of every poor person in the country. As soon as that was disposed of, another member brought forward a resolution that the Society should do its best to put the bible into the hands of every Slave in the country. That subject was discussed for two days, and at the end of that time they threw the resolution under the table, virtually resolving that they would not make an attempt to send bibles to the Slaves.

Leaving the American Bible Society, the next is the American Tract Society. What have you to say against the American Tract Society? you may ask. I have nothing to say against any association that is formed for a benevolent purpose, if it will only carry out the purpose for which it was formed. Has the American Tract Society ever published a single line against the sin of Slaveholding? You have all, probably, read tracts treating against licentiousness, against intemperance, against gambling, against Sabbath-breaking, against dancing, against almost every sin that you can think of; but not a single syllable has ever been published by the American Tract Society against the sin of Slaveholding. Only a short time since they offered a reward of $500 for the best treatise against the sin of dancing. A gentleman wrote the treatise, they awarded him the $500, and the tract is now in the course of publication if it is not already published. Go into a nice room, with fine music, and good company, and they will publish a tract against your dancing; while three millions are dancing every day at the end of the master's cowhide, and they cannot notice it! Oh, no; it is too small fry for them! They cannot touch that, but they can spend their money in publishing tracts against your dancing here at the North, while the Slave at the South may dance until he dances into his grave, and they care nothing for him. . . .

When I speak of Slavery I am carried back to the time when I saw, day after day, my own fellow countrymen placed upon the auction stand; when I saw the bodies, and sinews, and hearts, and the souls of men sold to the highest bidder. I have with me an account of a Slave recently sold upon the auction stand. The auctioneer could only get a bid of $400, but as he was about to knock her off, the owner of the Slave made his way through those that surrounded him and whispered to the auctioneer. As soon as the owner left, the auctioneer said, "I have failed to tell you all the good qualities of this Slave. I have told you that she was strong, healthy, and hearty, and now I have the pleasure to announce to you that she is very pious. She has got religion." And although, before that, he could only get $400, as soon as they found that she had got religion they commenced bidding upon her, and the bidding went up to $700. The writer says that her body and mind were sold for $400, and her religion was sold for $300. My friends, I am aware that there are people at the North who would sell their religion for a $5 bill, and make money on it; and that those who purchased it would get very much cheated in the end. But the piety of the Slave differs from the piety of the people in the nominally free States. The piety of the Slave is to be a good servant.

SOURCE: William Wells Brown, A *Lecturer Delivered before the Female Anti-Slavery Society of Salem* (Boston: Massachusetts Anti-Slavery Office, 1847), 4–6, 7, 9, 10–12, 21.

American Colorphobia (1847)

William Lloyd Garrison

Not all white abolitionists believed that the very slaves whose freedom they sought were their equals in intelligence or discipline. They were as susceptible, although to a lesser degree, to the infection of what William Lloyd Garrison here calls "colorphobia" as most other nine-teenth-century Americans. Garrison was one of the few white abolitionists who insisted that slavery and racism went hand in hand, and that both needed to be eradicated if justice were to reign.

In this essay, he deplores racism in a country that claims to be the "pattern-land of the world" when it comes to democracy and equal rights. It's not surprising, he continues, that many free blacks, including Frederick Douglass, opt to leave the United States if they are able for lands in which a dark complexion isn't a crime.

There is nothing which excites more unfeigned astonishment in the old world, than the prejudice which dogs the footsteps of the man of color in this pseudo republic. True, there are many absurd, criminal, aristocratic distinctions abroad, which ought to cease; but these are also found, to a great extent, in the United States, and have been common to all countries, and in every age. They originate in the pride of wealth, in successful enterprise, in educational superiority, in official rank, in civil, military, and ecclesiastical rule. For these, there may be framed some plausible excuses. But to enslave, brutalize, scorn and insult human beings solely on account of the hue of the skin which it has pleased God to bestow on them; to pronounce them accursed, for no crime on their part; to treat them substantially alike, whether they are virtuous or vicious, refined or vulgar, rich or poor, aspiring or groveling; to be inflamed with madness against them in proportion as they rise in self-respect, and improve in their manners and morals; this is an act so unnatural, a crime so monstrous, a sin so God-defying, that it throws into the shade all other distinctions known among mankind. Thank God, it is confined to a very small portion of the globe; though, strange to tell, it is perpetrated the most grossly, and in a spirit the most ferocious and inexorable, in a land claiming to be the pattern-land of the world—the most enlightened, the most democratic, the most Christian. Complexional caste is tolerated nowhere excepting in the immediate vicinage of slavery. It has no foundation in nature, reason, or universal custom. But, as the origin of it is to be traced to the existence of slavery, so its utter eradication is not to be expected until that hideous system be overthrown. Nothing but the removal of the cause can destroy the effect. That, with all its desperate efforts to lengthen its cords and strengthen its stakes, the Slave Power is continually growing weaker, is most clearly demonstrated in the gradual abatement of the prejudice which we have been deploring; for strong and terrible as that prejudice now is, it has received a very perceptible check within the last ten years, especially in New England.

No one can blame the intelligent and virtuous colored American for turning his back upon the land of his nativity, and escaping from it with the precipitancy that marked the flight of Lot out of Sodom. To remain in it is to subject himself to continual annoyance, persecution, and outrage. In fifteen or twenty days, he can place his feet on the shores of Europe—in Great Britain and Ireland—where, if he cannot obtain more food or better clothing, he can surely find that his complexion is not regarded as a crime, and constitutes no barrier to his social, intellectual, or political advancement. He who, with this powerful temptation to become an exile before him, is resolved to remain at home, and take his lot and portion with his downtrodden brethren—to lay his comfort, reputation, and hopes on the altar of freedom—exhibits the true martyr spirit, and is deserving of a world's sympathy and applause. Such a man, in eminent degree, is FREDERICK DOUGLASS. Abroad, beloved, honored, admitted to the most refined circles, and a host of Britain's highest intellects;—at home, not without numerous friends and admirers, it is true, yet made the object of popular contumely, denied the customary rights and privileges of a man, and surrounded by an atmosphere of prejudice which is enough to appall the stoutest heart, and to depress the most elastic spirit. Such is the difference between England and America; between a people living under a monarchial form of government, and a nation of boasting republicans!—O what crimes are perpetrated under the mask of democratic liberty! what outrages are consummated under the profession of Christianity!

> Fleecy locks and dark complexion
> Cannot forfeit Nature's claim;
> Skins may differ, but affection
> Dwells in white and black the same.

SOURCE: William Lloyd Garrison, "American Colorphobia," *The Liberator* (June 11, 1847).

Sermon to Medical Students (1849)

Lucretia Mott

Lucretia Mott (1793–1880) was one of the most formidable and influential American activists of the nineteenth century. A tireless proponent of both abolition and women's rights, she was a close associate of William Lloyd Garrison and co-organizer, with Susan B. Anthony, of the 1848 Seneca Falls convention for women's rights. Mott's dedication to both sprang from her Quaker conviction, as she states in this selection from one of her sermons, that the Kingdom of God (or what Quakers frequently call the "inner Light) is within each person. Consequently, the call to treat others with justice and compassion is a "self-evident" principle.

Here Mott urges young medical students to realize that their calling obliges them to care for the total well-being of persons, and that slavery is a grave impediment to both physical and spiritual health. Apparently, there were at least some students from slave states in her audience, because she encouraged them, when they returned home, not to legitimize slavery by "permission, apology, or otherwise." The published transcript of her remarks reveals that several of them got up and left in protest.

I called you not here for any theological discussion. The religion we profess—the principles of Christianity we believe it our duty in inculcate, are not wrapped in mystery, or in theories that are dividing and sub-dividing Christendom. In the view of many, the gospel is not preached, unless it embrace a certain scheme of salvation and plan of redemption. Faith in Christ has become so involved with a belief in human depravity and a vicarious atonement, imputed sin and imputed righteousness, that a discourse is divested of the character of gospel preaching, and regarded as little other than a mere lecture, if this scheme and plan—this system or theory, be not embraced.

I confess to you, my friends, that I am a worshipper after the way called heresy—a believer after the manner which many deem infidel. While, at the same time, my faith is firm in the blessed, the eternal doctrines preached by Jesus, and by every child of God from the creation of the world; especially the great truth that God is the teacher of his people himself; the doctrine that Jesus most emphatically taught, that the kingdom of God is within man—that there is his sacred and divine temple. This religious doctrine is simple, because it appeals to self-evident conviction. It is divested of mystery and mysticism, for it is not necessarily connected, with anything miraculous or extraordinary.

This noble gift of God, is as legitimate a part of man's being, as the moral sense with which he is quickened, the intellectual power with which he is so abundantly endowed, or as the animal propensities which are bestowed for his pleasure, his comfort, his good. All these are equally of divine origin. The religion offered to our acceptance tends in no wise to degrade man, to lessen his proper self-respect, or lead him to undervalue any of the gifts of the great Creator. I believe man is created innately good; that his instincts are for good. It is, by a perversion of these, through disobedience, that the purity of his soul becomes sullied. Rejecting, then, the doctrine of human depravity, denying that by nature we have wicked hearts, I have every confidence, every hope, in addressing an audience of unsophisticated minds, that they may be reached, because I know that the love of God has previously touched their hearts; that He has implanted there, a sense of justice and mercy, of charity and all goodness. This is the beauty and divinity of true religion, that it is universal. Wherever man is found, these great attributes of Deity are there found—a nice sense of justice, a quick perception of love, a keen apprehension of mercy, and of all the glorious attributes of God; without puzzling the mind with attempts to reconcile His imagined infinite justice, with his prescience or his infinite power.

Christianity has been lamentably marred in its glory and beauty, by the gloomy dogmas of the schools. Many, however, are now enquiring for themselves, and acknowledging the heavenly light within them. They begin to understand the divine mission of Jesus; how it is that his coming was and ever is to bless mankind, by turning everyone from his iniquities; that in him, in the great truths he preached, all nations shall be blessed.

In the exercise of the intellectual powers, in the advancement and discoveries in science, the vague theories of past ages are yielding to fact and demonstration, so as to require no dry argument to prove their truth to the hearer. So also in religion, the highest concern of man. Theories long held in darkness, are now brought to a strict examination; the people are exercising their rational powers, and bringing that which is offered them, to the light of truth in themselves. In this there is much to hope. The intelligent mind receiving truth in the obedience of a little child, comes to be quick in its perception and understanding, of all that belongs to the soul's salvation.

This is no mere Quaker doctrine. Certain also of your own writers bear this testimony: "All mysteries of science and theology fade away, before the grandeur of the simple perception of duty, which dawns on the mind of the little child. He becomes subject from that moment to a law which no power in the universe can abrogate. He hears a voice which, if faithfully followed, will lead him to happiness, and, in neglecting which, he brings upon himself inevitable misery."* This is the faith that we

---

*The quote is from Unitarian minister William Ellery Channing's sermon "Honor Due to All Men" in *Works* (London: Chapman, 1844), Vol. 1, p. 251. I've been unable to trace the author of the quotation immediately following.

preach. It commends itself to the understanding and heart of the hearer, bringing him to a close examination of his daily life and practice. Another writer has observed: "The divine principle in man is given, not for the gratification of our curiosity, but for the government of our lives." Were this kept in view, the tone of the preaching on this day of the week would be changed. Abstract theories, as well as the attempted descriptions of a future world, would give place to the enforcing of the great practical duties of life. For while any verbal or ceremonial standard shall obtain, as the essential of Christianity, the standard of pure morality and practical righteousness is proportionally lowered. Especially so, if the theory shall teach, that good works are of no avail, making a wide separation between faith and practice. We have not so learned Christ.

I would then urge upon your consideration how far you are faithful to that in your hearts, which you have felt to be near to you, in your solitary moments, when your prayer has ascended, as I doubt not it has at seasons, from the altar of every heart now present. When the quick response of the Father's love has shewn you in what your duty consists, how far, I would appeal to your best feelings, does your conscience acquit you, that you have been obedient to the heavenly vision, that you have confessed this divinity before men? Are ye willing to acknowledge to your companions, oh ye young men, that you cannot conscientiously do this, or are conscientiously bound to do that? Believe me, this confession of the Savior is of far more consequence to you, than a belief in a mysterious divinity. The divinity of Christ was not in mystery or miracle. It was in doing the will of his Father. He was "the son of God with power according to the spirit of holiness."

Cultivate this ennobling view; be obedient to the truth; so will you make advancement in your several neighborhoods and become wiser than your teachers. You will exalt the standard of justice and mercy above that around which your Fathers have rallied. One object in inviting you here this evening was, to speak plainly, as regards the prevailing errors and sins of the time....

Your growing knowledge of the system of man impresses the importance of observing every law of his physical being, in order to be preserved a perfect whole. The light of truth has revealed to you your noble powers, and the responsibility of exercising them in the purity with which they have been bestowed. If then by your studies you are made intelligently acquainted with these things, and if superadded, you have a quick sense of the divinity of the soul, responding to and according with this knowledge, how increasingly incumbent is it upon you to carry out your principles among your associates, so that you be not found in the background in the great reformation that is taking place in human society.

This is part of my religion—a part of true Christianity, and you must bear with me, my friends, if I press upon you duties, having reference to your different relations in society, to your intercourse with men, wherever you are placed.

It has been my privilege and pleasure to meet with some of you in our Anti-Slavery Rooms. When these have been disposed to come there, though perhaps from mere curiosity, to see what the despised abolitionist was doing, I have been glad to meet them, and to offer such considerations as would induce a reflection upon the relation which they bear to our fellow beings in their own country and neighborhood. This, in the view of many, is a subject of delicacy—lightly to be touched. Still it is an essential part of Christianity; and one object in asking your audience this evening, was to offer for your consideration some views connected with it, in the hope that you would at least patiently hear, and "suffer the word of exhortation."

There are many now looking at the subject of slavery in all its bearing, who are sympathizing with the condition of the poor and oppressed in our land. Although many of you may be more immediately connected with this system, yet it is coming to be regarded as not a mere sectional question, but a national and an individual one. It is interwoven throughout our country, into much with which we have to do, that we may well acknowledge we are all, all "verily guilty concerning our brother." There is, therefore, the greater responsibility that we first examine ourselves and ascertain what there is for us to do in order that we may speedily rid ourselves of the great evil that is clinging to us.

Evil—sin which so easily besets us. There are those here who have had their hearts touched, who have been led to feel and have entered into sympathy with the bondman, and have known where the evil lies. I believe there is a work for you to do, when you return home, if you will be faithful to yourselves. You will be brought more deeply to enter into feeling with the poor and oppressed slave; you will find that the mission of the gospel is "to bind up the broken hearted, to preach deliverance to the captive." It would be a reflection upon the intelligence and the conscience of those who are here, to suppose that they would always resist the wisdom and power with which truth is speaking to their hearts upon this subject. There are many disposed to examine, to cultivate their minds and hearts in relation to their duties in this respect. May you be faithful, and enter into a consideration as to how far you are partakers in this evil, even in other men's sins. How far, by permission, by apology, or otherwise, you are found lending your sanction to a system which degrades and brutalizes three millions of our fellow human beings; which denies to them the rights of intelligent education, rights essential to them, and which we acknowledge to be dear to us.

Is this an evil that cannot be remedied? A remedy is nigh at hand, even at the door. The voice has been heard saying, Proclaim liberty to the captive, the opening of the prison to them that are bound. Proclaim yet liberty throughout all the land unto all the inhabitants thereof. To this land peculiarly is this language applicable. In this land especially are we called to be faithful in this subject. Be true to your conviction of duty then, oh my brethren, and you will have the blessing of beholding your own country purged of the iniquity, and be brought to acknowledge that the divine hand of mercy and love has been stretched over our land.

*[Here a few persons, irritated by this reference to
the question of slavery, left the meeting.]*

It should not be strange that the allusion to this subject
should create some little agitation among you; and while I can
but regret it, I stand here on behalf of the suffering and the dumb,
and must express the desire, that there may be a disposition to
hear and reflect, and then judge. I speak unto those who have
ears to hear, who have hearts to feel. May their understandings
not be closed! May they be willing to receive that which conflicts
with their education, their prejudices and preconceived opinions.
The subject of slavery you must know, is now agitating the country from one end to the other. The Church and the Legislative
Hall are occupied with its discussion. It will be presented to you
in all its various bearings, and let me urge such faithfulness to the
light which you have, as shall prepare you to become able advocates for the oppressed. So shall the blessing descend upon you as
well as upon those for whom the appeal is made. I should not be
true to myself did I not thus urge this subject upon your consideration. When you have opportunities for meditation and reflection, when your feelings are soothed by the circumstances around
you, may you be led to reflect upon your duties, and the responsibility of your position in society.

SOURCE: Lucretia Mott, *A Sermon to Medical Students in Philadelphia*
(Philadelphia: Merrihew & Thompson, 1849), 6–11, 12–16.

Duty of Disobedience to Wicked Laws
(1851)

Charles Beecher

Brother of Harriet Beecher Stowe, Charles Beecher (1815–1900) pastored Newark, New Jersey's First Presbyterian (and later Congregationalist) Church throughout most of the 1850s. Under his leadership, it became one of the North's most outspokenly abolitionist congregations. At the end of the Civil War, Beecher and his wife relocated to Florida, where he became involved in educating former slaves.

In this sermon, preached after the passage of the 1850 Fugitive Slave Act, which required magistrates and citizens in free states to cooperate in the capture and return of runaway slaves, Beecher recommends—and, indeed, commands—civil disobedience to it. The Act, he insists, encourages "piracy" and "popery": the first a reference to the theft of freedom committed by slavery, the second the abdication of "liberty of conscience" and "right of private judgment" that obedience to the Act requires. Any law, argues Beecher, which commands people to "deny Christ" and "renounce Christ's law" is an abomination. The only thing worse than legislating such a law is obeying it.

This law is wrong in the sight of God and man—it is an unexampled climax of sin. It is the monster iniquity of the present age, and it will stand for ever on the page of history as the vilest monument of history of the nineteenth century. Russia knows nothing like it. Hungary blesses God that *she* never suffered anything worse than Haynau.* And nations afar off pause a while from their worship of blocks of wood and stone to ask: what will those Christians do next?

God from his throne, who beholds all the nations of the earth, looks down, and Christ who hungers and thirsts, is naked, sick, and in prison with one of the least of his brethren, looks down to see what gigantic culmination of guilt, what accumulation of shame and sin, is proceeding to its consummation; for I remark that there is yet one thing more guilty than the passing of this law. There is yet one step wanting to render complete and awful in the sight of God our mighty guilt; and that step is obedience to the law. That is a sin even more exquisitely sinful than the making of the law itself, for two reasons: first, because it has the whole atrociousness of the law itself; and secondly, because it has the whole atrociousness of a stab at the freedom of conscience, and of private judgment.

If this law is obeyed, what does a Christian do and why does he do it? I answer, he commits an act of piracy, and he does it because the law says so, and because he must obey the law right or wrong, as it is a law. These are the two elements of guilt in the obedience of this law: First, what it is; second, why it is. First, PIRACY; second, POPERY.

Why does any man imagine he ought to obey the law? What is the Jesuitical plea which is industriously inculcated by the high priests of Moloch and Mammon? It is because he wants to keep on the safe side by obeying law. Because he is told that the proper way is to obey, until the law can be altered. Because he is told it is wrong to do right, unless the Government gives him leave— right to do wrong, whenever an aristocracy of politicians, and a

---

*Julius Jacob von Haynau (1786–1853), an Austrian general whose notoriously cruel suppressions of insurrection in Hungary earned him the nickname of "the hangman of Arad" because of his execution of thirteen Hungarian rebel generals in the town of Arad following their surrender.

hierarchy of office holders, command. Because he pins his faith on the sleeve of Government, and makes Congress his pope, cardinals, and holy college of Jesuits, to act the part of infallible interpreter for him, of the Bible and of duty. This is the reason, and the only reason why he obeys. The law says so, and the law must be obeyed, right or wrong, till it is altered. Argument always used by Jesuits and despots, on weak consciences, and weaker brains. Argument first begotten of Satan, Father of Lies.

Let us picture to ourselves for a moment what is really contained in obedience to this law.

It is a Sabbath evening. It is winter, and the snow is on the ground, and the winds are out, filled with driving snow. You have just come from the communion table, with the taste of the bread and the touch of the wine upon your lips. The memory of Jesus thrills yet within your soul. You seem to hear those strange mysterious words: "This is my blood shed for you—This is my body broken for you." When, hark—upon the wild winter blast, a faint low cry meets your ear; a faint footstep approaches your door; a timid hand smites against your lintel. You rise from before your blazing fire, and look out into the night.

Feeble with hunger, ragged, with naked feet, pressing to her bosom, a pining infant, a mother totters before you, just sinking to the earth. "For the love of Jesus," she cries, "grant me a hiding place from my pursuers! Grant me a morsel of food! Save me, save my child, from a fate worse than death!"

That supplicant has known Jesus as well as you, and has, like you, tasted the sacred bread and wine. And she flies, a child of God, and an heir of heaven, she flies from a master, and from a system that would sink her to the depths of shame and licentious degradation.

What does this law require of you? What must you do, to obey this law? What is obedience to law? You must shut your door in her face, or you must take her captive, and shut her up until the hounds of officers can come up.

This is obedience; and if you do not do this you are a law breaker. If you give her a crust of bread, you break the law. If you give her a shawl, a cloak; if you let her warm herself by your fire an hour, and depart, you break the law. If you give her a night's rest, and let her go, you break the law. If you show her any kindness, any mercy, if you trust her as Christ trusted you, if you do to her as you would wish to be done by, you have broken the law.

Therefore you say to her, "My dear sister, I am sorry for you, but I cannot help you. If I let you in, I must keep you, and send for the officer; but I cannot help you any—the law says I must not, and my conscience will not let me disobey. Had you not better come in, and stay and be caught? Or would you rather go on?"

"Stay?—be caught!" groans the wretched mother. "No, never! Rather let me die! Rather let me lay my child cold and stiff in the snow wreath, for there at least we shall be free." She staggers away, her child uttering a faint moan. You shut your door, and sit down to read your Bible, saying, "Well, I have kept on the safe side; I have obeyed the law of my country." If it be objected that this is an extreme case, I deny it; the law makes no exceptions. This and nothing short of this, the law requires.

Here then is the sinfulness of obedience, viewed in the act itself; and I say, and every heart feels, that the sinfulness partakes of the guilt of murder. "He that seeth his brother suffer need, and shutteth up his bowels of compassion from him, how dwelleth the love of God in him?" [1 John 3:17]. "He that hateth his brother is a murderer, and ye know that no murderer hath eternal life abiding in him" [1 John 3:15]. And the act of obedience to this law is of its own nature murderous, malignant, and devilish.

But this is only one element of the guilt of obedience; the other element is the sacrifice of the right of private judgment, and of liberty of conscience.

"I know it is wrong, abstractly considered," you say, "but the law says so, and I must do it till the law is altered. True, it seems to me wrong, but what right have I to set up my judgment against the law? True, it seems to me that this law conflicts with the golden rule, on which hang all the Law and the prophets, and nullifies all principles of honor and humanity, but what right have I to follow my own private impression of right against the laws of the land? What right have I to say I will obey the laws of the land just so far as they coincide with my ideas of right, but when they do not, I will break them? If everybody should do so, would it not put an end to all law, and disorganize society? No, no; I must try to get this law repealed, but in the meanwhile I must keep it, even if it commands me to violate every principle of the Decalogue." Here is the stereotyped argument for all such cases made and provided, which has been used by civil and religious despotism in all ages. First pass a law that compels men to violate conscience, and then drive them to keep it by conscience. The worst of it is that these profligate preachers of integrity cheat their hearers by a fallacy, a falsehood so slyly slipped in, as to escape detection. They misrepresent the whole position of conscientious men. They represent us as if we claimed the right to violate any law that might happen not to suit our convenience, or our notions of propriety. They say that our claim of the right to violate one law, which we consider wrong, is a warrant for the violation of all laws, right or wrong. Now, this is a false conclusion. It represents us as confounding the distinction between laws which are simply injurious or inexpedient, and those which are positively sinful.

I may disapprove a law, I may think it unwise, injudicious, and even unjust in its bearings on me, and on my interests, and yet it may not require me to do anything positively wrong. I may submit to such a law, innocently, because I wrong nobody. But here is a law which commands me to sin positively and without apology. It commands me, when fully obeyed, to deny Christ, to renounce and abjure Christ's law, to trample under foot Christ's Spirit, and to remand Christ's flesh and blood into cruel bondage.

A law which does me some injury is one thing. A law which makes me do wrong is another. The first I may submit to while seeking its repeal. To the latter I must not give place by subjection, no, not for an hour. I must resist unto blood, striving against sin, i.e., to the patient shedding of my own blood. Hence, to disobey such a law does not disorganize society. It does not unsettle law.

The men that refuse obedience to such laws are the sure, the only defenders of law. If they will shed their own blood rather than sin by keeping a wicked law, they will by the same principle shed their blood rather than break a law which is righteous. In short, such men are the only true law-abiding men. For they never break a law, except when they see that to keep it would be to violate all law in its very foundation, and overturn the very government of God; while those men who clamor for blind obedience to all law—right or wrong—are striking at the throne of God.

Hence the principle involved in this discussion is not new. The question now is about obeying the law which repeals the golden rule....

The same principle was tried in the life of Christ. The Senate had made certain laws which this Galilean carpenter thought conflicted with the higher law of God. Those laws were not half so bad as this law of an American Congress, yet Christ broke them without scruple. Moreover, the Jewish State was a form of government directly instituted by God, even more than our own, so that if ever there was a case where the private citizen had no right to disobey for conscience sake, it was there. What right had he to tell those hoary rulers that they made void the law of God by their tradition, and taught for commandments the ordinance of men? Yet Jesus did this—he persisted in doing this; and when it came to the test whether he would obey them or God, he let them crucify him rather than yield. And God justified him in so doing by raising him from the dead.

The party that crucified Christ, and the party that are now ready to put to the bayonet all who disobey this wicked law, are one and the same; their maxims, spirit, arguments, and policy are the same. And their fate will be the same....

In conclusion, therefore, my application of the subject is— DISOBEY THE LAW. If you have ever dreamed of obeying it, repent before God, and ask his forgiveness. I counsel no violence. I suggest no warlike measures of resistance. I incite no man to deeds of blood. I speak as the minister of the Prince of Peace. As much as lieth in you, live peaceably with all men. To the fugitive, touching the question of self-defense, I offer no advice, as none can be necessary. The right of self-defense is unquestionable here, if ever. Of the expedience of its exercise, every man must judge for himself. Leave the question of self-defense undiscussed, to the settlement of every man's own judgment, according to circumstances.

But if a fugitive claims your help on his journey, break the law and give it hm. The law is broken as thoroughly by indirectly aiding his escape as directly, for both are penal. Therefore break the law, and help him on his way, directly if you can, indirectly if you must. Feed him, clothe him, harbor him, by day and by night, and conceal him from his pursuers and from the officers of the law. If you are summoned to aid in his capture, refuse to obey. If you are commanded by the officer to lay hands on the fugitive, decline to comply; rather, if possible, detain the officer, if you conveniently can, without injury to his person, until the victim is clean gone. If for these things you are accused and brought to trial, appear and defend yourself. If asked how you dared disobey the law of this realm, answer with Bunyan's Pilgrim in Vanity Fair.* Tell the court that you obey Christ, not Belial. If they fine you, and imprison you, take joyfully the spoiling of your goods,

---

*A reference to John Bunyan's 1678 *The Pilgrim's Progress*. Vanity Fair is a locale in the allegory inspired by the Book of Ecclesiastes' claim that "all is vanity."

wear gladly your chain, and in the last day you shall be rewarded for your fidelity to God. Do not think any true disgrace can attach to such penalties. It is the devil, and the devil's people only, who enact, enforce, or respect such penalties... To suffer is honor; to be defamed, reviled, and spit upon, is glory.

Source: Charles Beecher, *The Duty of Disobedience to Wicked Laws. A Sermon on the Fugitive Slave Law* (New York: John A. Gray, Printer, 1851), 13–16, 17, 21–22.

Caste and Christ (1852)

Harriet Beecher Stowe

Famously described by Abraham Lincoln as the "little woman who wrote the book that started this great war," Harriet Beecher Stowe (1811–1896), author of Uncle Tom's Cabin, *was a committed abolitionist who, along with her husband and three of her brothers, committed herself to the cause of abolitionism. It's arguable that her fictional depiction of the cruelty of slavery in her most famous novel was the most influential anti-slavery document written by an American. In "Caste and Christ," Stowe uses the anti-slavery slogan "Am I not a man and a brother?" as inspiration for her insistence that Christ sees no one as an outcast, especially because of skin color. Neither should Christians.*

Ho! thou dark and weary stranger
    From the tropic's palmy strand,
Bowed with toil, with mind benighted,
    What wouldst thou upon our land?

Am I not, O man, thy brother?
    Spake the stranger patiently,
All that makes thee, man, immortal,
    Tell me, dwells it not in me?

I, like thee, have joy, have sorrow,
    I, like thee, have love and fear,

I, like thee, have hopes and longings
    Far beyond this earthly sphere.

Thou art happy—I am sorrowing,
    Thou art rich, and I am poor;
In the name of our *one* Father
    Do not spurn me from your door.

Thus the dark one spake, imploring,
    To each stranger passing nigh,
But each child and man and woman,
    Priest and Levite passed him by.

Spurned of men—despised, rejected,
    Spurned from school and church and hall,
Spurned from business and from pleasure,
    Sad he stood, apart from all.

Then I saw a form all glorious,
    Spotless as the dazzling light,
As He passed, men veiled their faces,
    And the earth, as heaven, grew bright.

Spake he to the dusky stranger,
    Awe-struck there on bended knee,
Rise! For *I* have called thee *brother*,
    I am not ashamed of thee.

When I wedded mortal nature
    To my Godhead and my throne,
Then I made all mankind sacred,
    Sealed all human for mine own.

By Myself, the Lord of ages,
    I have sworn to right the wrong,

I have pledged my word, unbroken,
For the weak against the strong.

And upon my gospel banner
    I have blazed in light the sign,
He who scorns his lowliest brother,
    Never shall have hand of mine.

Hear the word!—who fight for freedom!
    Shout it in the battle's van!
Hope! For bleeding human nature!
    Christ the *God*, is Christ the *man!*

SOURCE: Julia Griffiths, ed., *Autographs for Freedom* (Boston: John P. Jewett, 1853), 4–6.

What to the Slave Is the Fourth of July?
(1852)

Frederick Douglass

The immediate cause of this blistering rebuke of American culture in general and Christianity in particular by pre-eminent abolitionist and ex-slave Frederick Douglass (1818–1895) was the widespread failure of churches to condemn the Fugitive Slave Act. Passed in 1850 in an attempt to mollify slaveholding states, the act stipulated that slaves who escaped to the North had to be returned to bondage and that both officials and citizens of free states were obliged, under penalty of law, to assist in their capture.

In this oration, delivered in Rochester, New York, to an anti-slavery gathering, Douglass argues that churches that fail to defy the law have blood on their hands, and points out the hypocrisy of American Christians who bemoan oppression in foreign lands while turning blind eyes to slavery in the United States.

I take this law to be one of the grossest infringements of Christian Liberty, and, if the churches and ministers of our country were not stupidly blind, or most wickedly indifferent, they, too, would so regard it.

At the very moment that they are thanking God for the enjoyment of civil and religious liberty, and for the right to worship God according to the dictates of their own consciences, they are utterly silent in respect to a law which robs religion of its chief significance, and makes it utterly worthless to a world lying in wickedness. Did this law concern the "mint, anise and cumin"— abridge the right to sing psalms, to partake of the sacrament, or to engage in any of the ceremonies of religion, it would be smitten by the thunder of a thousand pulpits. A general shout would go up from the church, demanding repeal, repeal, instant repeal! And it would go hard with that politician who presumed to solicit the votes of the people without inscribing this motto on his banner. Further, if this demand were not complied with, another Scotland would be added to the history of religious liberty, and the stern old Covenanters would be thrown into the shade. A John Knox would be seen at every church door, and heard from every pulpit, and Fillmore would have no more quarter than was shown by Knox, to the beautiful, but treacherous queen Mary of Scotland. The fact that the church of our country, (with fractional exceptions), does not esteem "the Fugitive Slave Law" as a declaration of war against religious liberty, implies that that church regards religion simply as a form of worship, an empty ceremony, and not a vital principle, requiring active benevolence, justice, love and good will towards man. It esteems sacrifice above mercy; psalm-singing above right doing; solemn meetings above practical righteousness. A worship that can be conducted by persons who refuse to give shelter to the houseless, to give bread to the hungry, clothing to the naked, and who enjoin obedience to a law forbidding these acts of mercy, is a curse, not a blessing to mankind. The Bible addresses all such persons as "scribes, Pharisees, hypocrites, who pay tithe of mint, anise, and cumin, and have omitted the weightier matters of the law, judgment, mercy and faith."

But the church of this country is not only indifferent to the wrongs of the slave, it actually takes sides with the oppressors. It has made itself the bulwark of American slavery, and the shield of American slave-hunters. Many of its most eloquent Divines ... [who] stand as the very lights of the church, have shamelessly given the sanction of religion and the Bible to the whole slave system. They have taught that man may, properly, be a slave; that the relation of master and slave is ordained of God; that to send back an escaped bondman to his master is clearly the duty of all the followers of the Lord Jesus Christ; and this horrible blasphemy is palmed off upon the world for Christianity.

For my part, I would say, welcome infidelity! Welcome atheism! Welcome anything! In preference to the gospel, as preached by those Divines! They convert the very name of religion into an engine of tyranny, and barbarous cruelty, and serve to confirm more infidels, in this age, than all the infidel writings of Thomas Paine, Voltaire, and Bolingbroke, put together, have done! These ministers make religion a cold and flinty-hearted thing, having neither principles of right action, nor bowels of compassion. They strip the love of God of its beauty, and leave the throng of religion a huge, horrible, repulsive form. It is a religion for oppressors, tyrants, man-stealers, and thugs. It is not that "pure and undefiled religion" which is from above, and which is "first pure, then peaceable, easy to be entreated, full of mercy and good fruits, without partiality, and without hypocrisy." But a religion which favors the rich against the poor; which exalts the proud above the humble; which divides mankind into two classes, tyrants and slaves; which says to the man in chains, stay there; and to the oppressor, oppress on; it is a religion which may be professed and enjoyed by all the robbers and enslavers of mankind; it makes God a respecter of persons, denies his fatherhood of the race, and tramples in the dust the great truth of the brotherhood of man. All this we affirm to be true of the popular church, and the popular worship of our land and nation—a religion, a church, and a worship which, on the authority of inspired wisdom, we pronounce to be an abomination in the sight of God. In the language of Isaiah, the American church might be well addressed, "Bring no more vain oblations; incense is an abomination unto me: the new moons and Sabbaths, the calling of assemblies, I cannot away with; it is iniquity even the solemn meeting. Your new moons and your appointed feasts my soul hateth. They are a trouble to me; I am weary to bear them; and when ye spread forth your hands I will hide mine eyes from you. Yea! When ye make many prayers, I will not hear. YOUR HANDS ARE FULL OF BLOOD; cease to do evil, learn to do well; seek judgment; relieve the oppressed; judge for the fatherless; plead for the widow" [Isaiah 1:13–17].

The American church is guilty, when viewed in connection with what it is doing to uphold slavery; but it is superlatively guilty when viewed in connection with its ability to abolish slavery. The sin of which it is guilty is one of omission as well as of commission. Albert Barnes but uttered what the common sense of every man at all observant of the actual state of the case will receive as truth, when he declared that "There is no power out of the church that could sustain slavery an hour, if it were not sustained in it."

Let the religious press, the pulpit, the Sunday school, the conference meeting, the great ecclesiastical, missionary, Bible and tract associations of the land array their immense powers against slavery and slave-holding; and the whole system of crime and blood would be scattered to the winds; and that they do not do this involves them in the most awful responsibility of which the mind can conceive.

In prosecuting the anti-slavery enterprise, we have been asked to spare the church, to spare the ministry; but how, we ask, could such a thing be done? We are met on the threshold of our efforts for the redemption of the slave, by the church and ministry of the country, in battle arrayed against us; and we are compelled to fight or flee. From what quarter, I beg to know, has proceeded a fire so deadly upon our ranks, during the last two years, as from the Northern pulpit? As the champions of oppressors, the chosen men of American theology have appeared: men, honored for their so-called piety, and their real learning [who] have, in utter denial of the authority of Him, by whom they profess to be called to the ministry, deliberately taught us, against the example or the Hebrews and against the remonstrance of the Apostles, they teach "that we ought to obey man's law before the law of God."

My spirit wearies of such blasphemy; and how such men can be supported, as the "standing types and representatives of Jesus Christ," is a mystery which I leave others to penetrate. In speaking of the American church, however, let it be distinctly understood that I mean the great mass of the religious organizations of our land. There are exceptions, and I thank God that there are, [men and women who] inspire our ranks with high religious faith and zeal, and cheer us on in the great mission of the slave's redemption from his chains....

Americans! Your republican politics, not less than your republican religion, are flagrantly inconsistent. You boast of your love of liberty, your superior civilization, and your pure Christianity, while the whole political power of the nation (as embodied in the two great political parties), is solemnly pledged to support and perpetuate the enslavement of three millions of your countrymen. You hurl your anathemas at the crowned headed tyrants of Russia and Austria, and pride yourselves on your Democratic institutions, while you yourselves consent to be the mere tools and bodyguards of the tyrants of Virginia and Carolina. You invite to your shores fugitives of oppression from abroad, honor them with banquets, greet them with ovations, cheer them, toast them, salute them, protect them, and pour out your money to them like water; but the fugitives from your own land you advertise, hunt, arrest, shoot and kill. You glory in your refinement and your universal education yet you maintain a system as barbarous and dreadful as ever stained the character of a nation—a system begun in avarice, supported in pride, and perpetuated in cruelty. You shed tears over fallen Hungary, and make the sad story of her wrongs the theme of your poets, statesmen and orators, till your gallant sons are ready to fly to arms to vindicate her cause against her oppressors; but, in regard to the ten thousand wrongs of the

American slave, you would enforce the strictest silence, and would hail him as an enemy of the nation who dares to make those wrongs the subject of public discourse! You are all on fire at the mention of liberty for France or for Ireland; but are as cold as an iceberg at the thought of liberty for the enslaved of America. You discourse eloquently on the dignity of labor; yet, you sustain a system which, in its very essence, casts a stigma upon labor. You can bare your bosom to the storm of British artillery to throw off a threepenny tax on tea; and yet wring the last hard-earned farthing from the grasp of the black laborers of your country. You profess to believe "that, of one blood, God made all nations of men to dwell on the face of all the earth," and hath commanded all men, everywhere to love one another; yet you notoriously hate, (and glory in your hatred), all men whose skins are not colored like your own. You declare, before the world, and are understood by the world to declare, that you "hold these truths to be self-evident, that all men are created equal; and are endowed by their Creator with certain inalienable rights; and that, among these are, life, liberty, and the pursuit of happiness"; and yet, you hold securely, in a bondage which, according to your own Thomas Jefferson, "is worse than ages of that which your fathers rose in rebellion to oppose," a seventh part of the inhabitants of your country....

Fellow-citizens! I will not enlarge further on your national inconsistencies. The existence of slavery in this country brands your republicanism as a sham, your humanity as a base pretense, and your Christianity as a lie. It destroys your moral power abroad; it corrupts your politicians at home. It saps the foundation of religion; it makes your name a hissing, and a by word to a mocking earth. It is the antagonistic force in your government, the only thing that seriously disturbs and endangers your Union. It fetters your progress; it is the enemy of improvement, the deadly foe of education; it fosters pride; it breeds insolence; it promotes vice; it shelters crime; it is a curse to the earth that supports it; and yet, you cling to it, as if it were the sheet anchor of all your hopes. Oh! Be warned! Be warned! A horrible reptile is coiled up in your nation's bosom; the venomous creature is nursing at the tender breast of your youthful republic; for the love of God, tear away, and fling from you the hideous monster, and let the weight of twenty millions crush and destroy it forever!

SOURCE: Frederick Douglass, *Oration, Delivered in Corinthian Hall, Rochester* (Rochester, NY: Lee, Mann & Co., 1852), 27–32, 34–35.

Guilt Modified by Ignorance (1852)

Charles Finney

A leader in the revivalist movement known as the Second Great Awakening and president of Oberlin College, a major waystation on the Underground Railroad, Charles Finney (1793–1875) saw the passage of the 1850 Fugitive Slave Act as an unholy law that threatened, as he says in this sermon, to turn the entire nation into a slave state.

He compares slavery here to temperance. Just as humans were once ignorant of the sinfulness of excessive drinking, so many Americans in the past were ignorant of the sinfulness of slavery. But once "growing light"—by which Finney means moral and religious illumination expressed in the abolitionist movement—pointed out the wickedness of human bondage, repentance and reformation ought to follow, just as it did when the temperance movement shed light on the truth about drinking. To persevere in slavery despite an awareness of its sinfulness "must hasten the destruction of a nation or people." Finney suspected that destruction wasn't far off. Civil war less than a decade later proved him right.

"And the times of this ignorance God winked at, but now commandeth all men everywhere to repent"—Acts 17:30.

When we use this language—wink at a thing—we mean, Let it pass with slight notice—let it go. Such must have been Paul's meaning. The principle assumed is as I have said, a well-established one—that men are guilty, or not guilty, or as the case may be, are more or less guilty, according to the knowledge they have or do not have, of their duty.

Applying this well-established principle, which all men hold and must hold, I remark, that since my recollection, a vast amount of light has been thrown on many great moral questions, and consequently the conduct of men in reference to the points they involve has assumed very different shades of moral character. For example, the question of Temperance. I can well remember when ministers used to drink before they went into the pulpit and drink after they came out of it. The same practices still continue in other countries. Then they thought it no wrong, unless they drank to excess, and beyond their own convictions of right. They measured their ideas of its harm by their own standard. But now so much light is abroad that the moral character of rum-drinking is essentially modified. In those very places where men drank without much guilt, they can no longer drink at all without great guilt. Then men were often advised to drink by their physicians. They thought they ought to drink for the sake of health. But this apology is available no longer. Why not? Because men have learned that health does not demand rum-drinking. They now know that it is wrong to use ardent spirits as a beverage, and that very rarely indeed does it need to be used as a medicine. Of course they cannot use the article as of old without great guilt—without losing every particle of their piety.

So on the subject of slavery. For a long time this subject was scarcely discussed at all. Slavery was abolished so quietly and gradually in the Northern States, that but little general discussion was excited. Yet the manner of its abolition in the North left the impression that Northern men had nothing to do with its abolition in the South. The work having been achieved by state legislative action, and without much of any foreign influence of any sort, it was not unnaturally assumed that other states would abolish slavery in the same way. Indeed, so little attention was given to this subject by Northern men, that they did not notice the gradual encroachments of the slave power upon the general government. But this state of things has greatly changed. Now men generally understand the relations of slavery to the national government. The startling fact is but too apparent that our Union is virtually a slaveholding state, and that Congress have seriously undertaken to make the entire domain of our country a slaveholding land. They enact their Fugitive Slave Bill into so-called law, and then send their commissioned agents into the free states, upon free soil, to compel free men, whose souls abhor slavery, to become slave-catchers, and to deliver up unto their masters or claimants, the servant that has escaped—in the very face of God's own command to the contrary, not to say also in the very face of every dictate of humanity. When the Northern states set their own slaves free, they had no thought of ever being dragged thus into the support of slavery. They expected, and were authorized to expect that the example of emancipation would be followed by the Southern states.

But instead of this, what do we see? Laws enacted by Congress which people all the free states with commissioners authorized to seize men as slaves—which deny them a jury trial and the right of habeas corpus—which leave them only the miserable mockery of the forms of trial, and which then, under heavy pains and penalties, compel us to sustain all this iniquity, and aid in dragging the arrested victim into hopeless bondage. I do not want to rail—you who hear me preach so often know full well that I am not; nor do I mean to rail on the worst of men or the most oppressive of their measures now; but the question what we, as men, shall do under this monstrous oppression is really momentous. The question now has taken this form; shall we individually and personally aid in making men slaves? This makes a solemn issue. I feel it to be such. . . .

Repentance is turning the heart to God, and abandoning selfishness. The work of repentance belongs to the heart or will. Of course it must be the function of the voluntary or moral department of the mind's powers.

But especially let me remark, that where repentance is genuine, there will be and must be external reformation. Men may have emotions of sorrow, with no change of purpose; but this is not real repentance.

Because as soon as we get light on any former practice which shows us that it is opposed to God's will, we cannot persist in it without greatly augmented guilt. For example, the case of intemperance. As soon as increasing light on this subject showed the extent of its mischiefs, and the absence of any and all redeeming good, the practice of using intoxicating drink as a beverage came to be seen at once as the murder of a man's own body and soul, and as a fatal temptation to his neighbor. Then, how could any man persist longer in its use without damning sin?

So of slavery. As soon as light prevails on this subject, men can no longer go on in the same course of sustaining the system, without the greatest guilt. It will not answer to substitute evasions, and dodging and side issues in place of real repentance and true reform. To evade the claims of truth thus serves not to acquit the soul before God or man, but only to strengthen depravity and harden the heart...

Refusal to repent when light reveals sin and duty, must hasten the destruction of any nation or people under heaven... The governments of the earth, if they resist the light that breaks in upon them, are sure to be destroyed. Who has not looked with admiration upon the English government, and marked its course when pressed by public sentiment to adopt demanded reforms? Their history for centuries is a series of triumphs achieved by the growing intelligence, firmness and wisdom of the people, calling for reforms in government or in the social condition of the masses. We can all of us remember the agitation long and deep which preceded the glorious act of West India emancipation.* If the government had withstood that appeal and refused to emancipate, I believe the refusal must have crushed the very throne itself. The people demanded the reform. The pulpit thundered and lightened—the whole public mind rocked as with the upheavings of an earthquake. The only safety lay in yielding to their demands.

No Christian nation since the world began has been able to stand against the united prayers and testimony of God's church.

---

*A reference to the Haitian Revolution in the "West Indies," which began in 1791 and ended in 1804 with independence and the abolition of slavery on the island.

No one has had strength to resist any reform which God's people have unitedly demanded. If they were seriously to determine on resistance, they would find God himself arrayed against them. O how would He drive his judgment-chariot, axle-deep in their blood and bones! Let his people stand on his side and do his work; they may expect his interposing arm for their support, crowning their toils with glorious victory. This must be so, by a law as undeviating and unfailing as the veracity of Jehovah!

This principle applies to all organizations, benevolent or ecclesiastical. If they resist reform when growing light demands it, God will be against them, and his chariot will grind them to powder! What does he want of a church or a benevolent society that resists reform when light and truth demand it, and sets itself in array against the progress of his cause? He knows how to use them for beacons of warning if they refuse to be used as instruments of progress in doing good. Therefore if any people or associate body will not receive and obey the light, their ruin is sure. The best of all possible reasons for repentance is, that it is God's good pleasure. What! If the expression of God's will—if the manifestation of his wishes to this effect cannot move men to repent, what can? What would you think of a child who should say, "No matter what my parents think—who cares for their feelings or their wishes? It is no reason at all for my conduct that my father or mother desire me to do as they say." What, I ask, would you think of such a child? Can anything be more monstrous than such a trampling underfoot of the most tender and sacred obligations?

Is it then no reason for you who are before me here to-day that God now commands you all to repent? Nay, more, that with tenderness he invites and entreats, and cries out, "How can I give thee up?"

SOURCE: Charles Finney, "Guilt Modified by Ignorance" (1852). Sermon Index.net. http://www.sermonindex.net/modules/articles/index.php?view=category&cid=96&page=2.

No Compromise with the Evil of Slavery
(1854)

William Lloyd Garrison

*Although always a religious man, Garrison grew more and more crit-
ical of institutional Christianity over the years because of what he saw
as its general refusal to condemn slavery. In this essay he thunders that
any religion which defends human bondage is in fact "atheistical" and
"the embodiment of all criminality." "The culprit here is a spirit of
compromise, especially evident in the northern free states, which is
willing to tolerate evil for the sake of expediency and profit. But once
it is admitted that biblically all people, regardless of their race, are
equally children of God, such compromise when it comes to slavery is
revealed for the abomination it is."*

The Abolitionism which I advocate is as absolute as the Law of
God, and as unyielding as His throne. It admits of no compromise. Every slave is a stolen man; every slaveholder is a man-
stealer. By no precedent, no example, no law, no compact, no
purchase, no bequest, no inheritance, no combination of circumstances, is slaveholding right or justifiable. While a slave remains
in fetters, the land must have no rest. Whatever sanctions his
doom must be pronounced accursed. The law that makes him a
chattel is to be trampled underfoot; the compact that is formed at
his expense, and cemented with his blood, is null and void; the
church that consents to his enslavement is horribly atheistical;
the religion that receives to its communion the enslaver is the
embodiment of all criminality.

Such, at least, is the verdict of my own soul, on the supposition that I am to be the slave; that my wife is to be sold from me for the vilest purposes; that my children are to be torn from my arms, and disposed of to the highest bidder, like sheep in the market. And who am I but a man? What right have I to be free, that another man cannot prove himself to possess by nature? No man is to be injured in his person, mind, or estate. He cannot be, with benefit to any other man, or to any state of society. Whoever would sacrifice him for any purpose is both morally and politically insane. Every man is equivalent to every other man. Destroy the equivalent, and what is left of "So God created man in his own image—male and female created he them" [Genesis 1:27]. This is a death-blow to all claims of superiority, to all charges of inferiority, to all usurpation, and to all oppressive dominion. No man can show that I have taken one step beyond the line of justice, or forgotten the welfare of the master, in my anxiety to free the slave....

If the slaves are not men; if they do not possess human instincts, passions, faculties and powers; if they are below accountability and devoid of reason; if for them there is no hope of immortality, no God, no heaven, no hell; if, in short they are, what the Slave Code declares them to be, rightly "deemed, sold, taken, reputed and adjudged in law to be chattels personal in the hands of their owners and possessors, and their executors, administrators and assigns, to all intents, constructions, and purposes whatsoever"; then, undeniably, I am mad, and can no longer discriminate between a man and a beast. But, in that case, away with the horrible incongruity of giving them oral instruction, of teaching them the catechism, or recognizing them as suitably qualified to be members of Christian churches, of extending to them the ordinance of baptism, and admitting them to the communion table, and enumerating many of them as belonging to the household of faith! Let them be no more included in our religious sympathies or denominational statistics than are the dogs in our streets, the swine in our pens, or the utensils in our dwellings. It is right to own, to buy, to sell, to inherit, to breed, and to control them, in the most absolute sense. All constitutions and laws which forbid their possession ought to be so far modified or repealed as to concede the right.

But, if they are men; if they are to run the same career of immortality with ourselves, if the same law of God is over them as over all others; if they have souls to be saved or lost; if Jesus includes them among those for whom he laid down his life; if Christ is within many of them the hope of glory, then, when I claim for them all that we claim for ourselves, because we are created in the image of God, I am guilty of no extravagance, but am bound, by every principle of honor, by all the claims of human nature, by obedience to the Almighty God, to remember them that are in bonds as bound with them, and to demand their immediate and unconditional emancipation....

How has the slave system grown to its present enormous dimensions? Through compromise. How is it to be exterminated? Only by an uncompromising spirit. This is to be carried out in all the relations of life—social, political, religious. Whatever may be the guilt of the South, the North is still more responsible for the existence, growth, and extension of slavery. In her hand has been the destiny of the Republic from the beginning. She could have emancipated every slave, long ere this, had she been upright in heart and free in spirit. She has given respectability, security, and the means of sustenance and attack to her deadliest foe. She has educated the whole country, and particularly the Southern portion of it, secularly, theologically, religiously; and the result is three millions and a half of slaves, increasing at the appalling rate of one hundred thousand a year, three hundred a day, and one every five minutes, the utter corruption of public sentiment, and general skepticism as to the rights of man. The pulpits, with rare exceptions, [are] filled with men as careful to consult the popular will as though there were no higher law....

While the present union exists, I pronounce it hopeless to expect any repose, or that any barrier can be effectually raised, against the extension of slavery. With two thousand million dollars' worth of property in human flesh in its hands, to be watched and wielded as one vast interest for all the South, with forces never divided, and purposes never conflictive, with a spurious, Negro-hating religion universally diffused, and everywhere ready to shield it from harm, with a selfish, sordid, divided North, long since bereft of its manhood, to cajole, bribe and intimidate, with its foot planted on two-thirds of our vast national domains, and there unquestioned, absolute and bloody in its sway, with the terrible strength and boundless resources of the whole country at its command, it cannot be otherwise than that the Slave Power will consummate its diabolical purposes to the uttermost....

What then, is to be done? Friends of the slave, the question is not whether by our efforts we can abolish slavery, speedily or remotely, for duty is ours, the result with God; but whether we will go with the multitude to do evil, sell our birthright for a mess of pottage, cease to cry aloud and spare not, and remain in Babylon when the command of God is, "Come out of her, my people" [Revelation 18:4].

SOURCE: William Lloyd Garrison, *No Compromise with Slavery: An address delivered to the Broadway Tabernacle* (New York: American Anti-Slavery Society, 1854), 14, 17–19, 21, 30–31, 35–36.

How Can I Help to Abolish Slavery? or, Counsels to the Newly Converted (1855)

Maria Weston Chapman

In this manifesto in support of the American Anti-Slavery Society, Maria Chapman (1806–1885) calls abolitionism "the great work of Christianity in our age and country." It was certainly a cause to which she dedicated a good part of her life. Based in Boston, she agitated under the auspices of the Massachusetts Anti-Slavery Society and the New England Anti-Slavery Society as well as the American Anti-Slavery Society. She spoke frequently and was an author and editor of abolitionist pamphlets and newspapers.

Here, Chapman discusses and rejects several strategies for addressing slavery that differ from the immediate emancipation she favored. The scheme to colonize ex-slaves in Liberia she condemns as both racist and impractical. Political solutions just kick the slavery can down the road. Buying slaves to free them is uneconomical and slow. Forming vigilance committees to aid runaway slaves requires secrecy, and secrecy in turn suggests that helping slaves escape is shameful. Education might persuade the mind but doesn't necessarily touch the heart or move the will. Finally, refusing to buy any goods not made by free labor salves the conscience but does little to end human bondage. What's necessary is to strike without compromise at the very existence of slavery.

Yes, my friend, I can resolve your question. Twenty years of actual experience qualify one to reply. I have stood, as you now stand, on the threshold of this grandest undertaking of any age—this effort to elevate a whole people in the scale of moral being—with my head full of plans, and my heart of devotedness, asking the same question. I really longed for this coming of millennial glory, and therefore soon found the road on which to go forth to meet it. My disgust was unutterable, as yours, too, will be, if you desire the abolition of slavery more than the temporary triumph of sect or party; at the stupid schemes by which selfish men were then, as now, trying to make capital for themselves out of the sacred cause of human rights—seeking to sell the gift of the Holy Ghost for money. Hear them clamorously and meanly taking advantage of innocence, for the promotion of self-interest.

First, hear the agents of slavery presenting the colonization scheme as the instrument of abolition.

"Aid the Colonization Society." Yes; to make slavery stronger by exalting prejudice as an ordination of divine Providence; to make slavery safer by eliminating that dangerous element, the free black; to make its term longer by stultifying national conscience. See that society making laws of slave States more cruel, the men of the free states more obdurate, the situation of the free men of color more difficult and insupportable, as a part of its plan. It could not, if it would, transport three millions of souls to Africa; the navies and revenues of the world would be insufficient. It would not, if it could; for slavery has no intention of parting with its three millions of victims; unless induced to free them out of generosity, it will keep them on speculation. Its forty years of colonization labor, and its million of gold and silver, have exiled fewer to Liberia than have escaped into Canada in spite of it—less in that period than the monthly increase of the slaves! It can do nothing for Christianizing Africa, for it sends a slaveholding gospel, which is anti-Christ. Be not deceived, then, by a tyrannical mockery like this, working to perpetuate slavery, and not to abolish it. Aid the American Anti-Slavery Society, which deals with the heart and conscience of this slaveholding nation, demanding immediate, unconditional emancipation; the abolition of slavery by the spirit of repentance, in conformity with all your own principles and traditions, whether religious or political.

Hear another cry, (coming, not like the first, from the enemies of abolition, but from friends, generally those of more pretension than devotedness): "Form a political party, free soil or other, to vote down slavery."

Yes, don't kill the growing monster—call to him to stop growing; merge immediatism, which always succeeds, in gradualism, which never does. Substitute a secondary object for the primary one. Strive in the first place not to abolish slavery, but to get one set of men out of office and another in, to learn by the event that the last are as incapable to turn back the whirlpool that masters the government as the first were. Make an appeal to force of numbers in a case where you know it is against you; in a case, too, where, having sworn assistance, you must lose influence by such an appeal. Spend your time and money, not in making new abolitionists, but in counting the old ones, that at every count diminish. Politics, in the common, small sense of the term, merely takes the circumstances it finds, and does its best with them. But the present circumstances are unfavorable. THEN CREATE NEW ONES. This is true politics, in the enlarged, real meaning of the word. Here is a building to be erected, and no sufficient materials. A little mortar, a few unbaked bricks—that is all. Go to the deep quarries of the human heart, and make of your sons and daughters polished stones to build the temple of the Lord. It is this cleaving into the living rock the AMERICAN ANTI-SLAVERY SOCIETY girds itself to do. Under its operations men become better and better abolitionists. Under the labors of political partisanship they necessarily grow worse and worse. They must ever ask themselves how little anti-slavery feeling and principle they can make serve the temporary turn; because the less of either, the greater the chance. They must always be sacrificing the end to the means. Call them to the witness box in the capacity of philosophical observers, and out of their little circumventing political characters, and themselves will tell you that the effect of electioneering on anti-slavery is most unfavorable, adding to the existing opposition to right the fury of party antagonism, throwing away the balance of power, lowering the tone of moral and religious feeling and action, and thus letting a sacred enterprise degenerate into a scramble for office. But labor with the AMERICAN ANTI-SLAVERY SOCIETY directly to the great end, and even Franklin Pierce and Co., pro-slavery as they are, will grovel to do your bidding. The administration now on the throne is as good for your bidding as any other. In a republican land the power behind the throne is the power. Save yourself the trouble of calling caucuses, printing party journals, distributing ballots, and the like. Let men who are fit for nothing of more consequence do this little work, which is best done by mere nobodies. More than enough of them are always ready for it. You, who are smitten by the sacred beauty of the great cause, should serve it greatly. Don't drag the engine, like an ignoramus, but bring wood and water and flame, like an engineer. The AMERICAN ANTI-SLAVERY SOCIETY has laid the track.

"Buy the slaves and set them free." Yes; lop the branches and strengthen the root; make the destruction of the system more difficult by practicing upon it; create a demand for the slave breeder to supply; compromise with crime; raise the market price, when you ought to stop the market; put a philanthropic mark upon the slave trade; spend money enough in buying one man to free fifty gratis, and convert a thousand. But there is a wholesale way, cries one. "Sell the public lands, and set every means in motion, from the merely mercantile donation of a million to the infant cent society, and thus raise two thousand millions of dollars, and beg the slaveholders to take it (not as compensation, but as a token of good will,) and let their bondmen go." I marvel at this insufficient notion of the heart of a slaveholder. I wonder exceedingly at such a want of imagination. "Not as compensation" is well put; for what sum can compensate a monarch for his throne? This system of slavery makes the south the parent of long lines of princes. It gives to her diabolical dominions

"Kingdoms, and sway, and strength, and length of days."

I am strangely divided in sympathy. I feel at once the generosity of the proposal, and have the feeling of contempt with which its insufficient inappropriateness is received.

"Organize vigilance committees, and establish underground railroads." Yes; hide from tyranny, instead of defying it: whisper a testimony; form a bad habit of mind in regard to despotism; try to keep out the sea with a mop, when you ought to build a dike; flatter your sense of compassion by taking private retail measures to have suffering ameliorated, when you might, with the AMERI-CAN ANTI-SLAVERY SOCIETY, be taking public wholesale measures to have the wrong (the cause of suffering) righted. You may safely leave with the half and quarter converted, with the slaveholders, the charge of all these things, which with the American Anti-Slavery Society are but as hydrogen and nitrogen without oxygen, however good with it, as the natural fruits of its labors. What I would discourage is, not mercy and compassion in an individual case, but a disgraceful mistake in the economy of well doing; spending in salving a sore finger what would buy the elixir vitae; preferring the less, which excludes the greater, to the greater, which includes the less. Slavery can only be abolished by raising the character of the people who compose the nation; and that can be done only by showing them a higher one. Now, there is one thing that can't be done in secret: you can't set a good example under a bushel.

"But instruction! Instruction! Found schools and churches for the blacks, and thus prepare for the abolition of slavery." O, shallow and shortsighted! The demand is the preparation; nothing can supply the place of that. And exclusive instruction, teaching for blacks, a school founded on color, a church in which men are herded ignominiously, apart from the refining influence of association with the more highly educated and accomplished,— what are they? A direct way of fitting white men for tyrants, and black men for slaves. No; if you would teach and Christianize the nation, strengthen the AMERICAN ANTI-SLAVERY SOCI- ETY, the only American institution founded on the Christian and republican idea of the equal brotherhood of man, and in op- position to a church and state which deny human brotherhood by sanctioning slavery, and pull down Christ to their own level. The American Anti-Slavery Society is church and university, high school and common school to all who need real instruction and true religion. Of it what a throng of authors, editors, lawyers, or- ators, and accomplished gentlemen of color have taken their de- gree! It has equally implanted hopes and aspirations, noble thoughts and sublime purposes in the hearts of both races. It has prepared the white man for the freedom of the black man, and it has made the black man scorn the thought of enslavement, as does a white man, as far as its influence has extended. Strengthen that noble influence. Before its organization, the country only saw here and there in slavery some "faithful Cudjoe or Dinah," whose strong natures blossomed even in bondage, like a fine plant beneath a heavy stone. Now, under the elevating and cher- ishing influence of the American Anti-Slavery Society, the col- ored race, like the white, furnishes Corinthian capitals for the noblest temples. Aroused by the American Anti-Slavery Society, the very white men who had forgotten and denied the claim of the black man to the rights of humanity now thunder that claim at every gate, from cottage to capitol, from school house to uni- versity, from the railroad carriage to the house of God. He has a place at their firesides, a place in their hearts—the man whom they once cruelly hated for his color. So feeling, they cannot send him to Coventry with a hornbook in his hand, and call it instruc- tion! They inspire him to climb to their side by a visible acted gospel of freedom. Thus, instead of bowing to prejudice, they conquer it.

"Establish free-labor warehouses." Indeed! Is that a good business calculation that leads to expend in search of the products of free labor the time and money that would make all labor free? While wrong exists in the world, you cannot (short of suicide) but draw your every life breath in involuntary connection with it; nor is conscience to be satisfied with anything short of a complete devotion to the anti-slavery cause of the life that is sustained by slavery. We may draw good out of evil: we must not do evil, that good may come. Yet I counsel you to honor those who eat no sugar, as you ask no questions for conscience's sake; while you despise those who thrust forward such a call upon conscience, impossible, in the nature of things, to be obeyed, and therefore not binding, as if it were the end of the law for righteousness, in order to injure Garrison, the great and good founder of the American Anti-Slavery Society. I have seen men drawing bills of exchange between England and the United States, while uttering maledictions against the American Anti-Slavery Society, because it does not, as such, occupy itself with the free produce question. This I brand as pro-slavery in disguise—sheer hypocrisy.

You see, my friend, that I have replied to your question in the conviction that you desire the abolition of slavery above all other things in this world; as one assured that it is the great work of Christianity in our age and country, as the conflict with idolatry was in other times and climes. Thus you see the salvation of the souls, the maintenance of the rights, the fulfillment of the duties, and the preservation of the free institutions of Americans to depend upon the extirpation of this accursed and disgraceful disease which is destroying them. If I had reason to think you merely desirous to make sectarian and political capital out of a holy thought and a sacred purpose originated by others—if you were merely contriving defenses for what is indefensible, and trying to save the credit of what is disgraceful, trying to throw dust, and change the issue, and pay tithes of cumin to delay justice, in order to spare your own insignificant self in this greatest conflict of light and darkness, good and evil, which the world has now to show—if you had been trying how to seem creditably interested in what ought to be an American's first business, and calculating how little instead of how much you might sacrifice to the soul-exalting cause of freedom—if you were the hired agent of some demisemiquaver of a movement which tacked anti-slavery to its other titles, in order to establish a claim on the purses of abolitionists—in any of these cases I would not have stopped to talk with you. Your interest being the thing you had at heart, I should not counsel; I should be called, in name of all that is holy, to condemn you, in order that blame might awake conscience. But the case, I trust, is different. I may, then, say to you, with all the confidence, nay, certainty, which is inseparable from experience, knowledge, and utter self-abnegation in the matter, WORK WITH THE AMERICAN ANTI-SLAVERY SOCIETY. Lavish your time, your money, your labors, your prayers, in that field, which is the world, and you will reap a thousandfold, now and hereafter. This movement moves. It is alive. Hear how everything mean and selfish struggles, hisses, and dies under its influence. Never, since the world was, has any effort been so clear, so strong, so uncompromising, so ennobling, so holy, and, let me add, so successful. It is "the bright consummate flower" of the Christianity of the nineteenth century. Look at those who "have not resisted the heavenly vision" it presented them of a nation overcoming its evil propensities, and doing right at all risks; ask them whether it has not saved their souls alive; ask them if it has not made them worshippers of the beauty and sublimity of high character, till they are ready to "know nothing on earth but Jesus Christ and him crucified." For this they give all—wealth, youth, health, strength, life. Worldly success, obtained by slackening their labors against slavery, (and it is easy to have it on those terms at any moment, so placable a monster is the world,) strikes them like failure and disgrace. They have "scorned delights, and lived laborious days," till at length they feel it no sacrifice, but

the highest joy. All this the American Anti-Slavery Society demands of you. DO IT! And be most grateful for the opportunity
of fulfilling a work which is its own exceeding great reward. DO
IT, and find yourself the chosen of God, to keep alive in this nation, degraded and corrupted by slavery, the noble flame of Christian faith, the sentiment of honor and fidelity, the instinct of
high-mindedness, the sense of absolute, immutable duty, the
charm of chivalrous and poetic feeling, which would make of the
poorest Americans the Christian gentlemen of the world.

> "Cherish all these high feelings that become
> A giver of the gift of liberty."

You will find yourself under the necessity of doing it in this noble
company, or alone. Try it. Strive to be perfect, as God is perfect—
to act up to your own highest idea, in connection with church or
state in this land corrupted by slavery, and see if you are helped
or hindered. Be not dragged along by them protesting. It is grac-
ing as a slave the chariot wheels of a triumph. But flee from them,
as one flees out of Babylon. Secure the blessing of union for good,
and be delivered from the curse of union in evil, by acting with
the AMERICAN ANTI-SLAVERY SOCIETY, its members and
friends.

I used this mode of expression advisedly, for I am not speaking of a mere form of association. Many are in harmonious cooperation with it who have neither signed the constitution nor
subscribed the annual half dollar. Hence it is neither a formality
nor a ceremony, but a united, onward-flowing current of noble
lives.

If, then, you feel that devotedness of heart which I verily
think your question indicates, I feel free to counsel you to go immediately to the nearest office of the American Anti-Slavery Society, by letter, if not in person, subscribe what money you can
afford—the first fruits of a life-long liberality, and study the cause
like a science, while promoting it like a gospel, under the cheer-

ing and helpful sympathy of some of the best company on earth: but not unless; for this company despises what politicians, ecclesiastical and other, call "getting people committed." They have a horror of this selfish invasion of another's freedom, as of the encumbrance of selfish help. They warn you not to touch the ark with unhallowed hands.

One consideration more—the thought of what you owe to your forerunners in what you feel to be the truth. It is, to follow meekly after, and be baptized with the baptism that they are baptized with. "Thus it becometh us to fulfil all righteousness": and the more your talents, gifts, and graces may, in your judgment, be superior to theirs, the more becoming it will be to seek their fellowship: for in the whole land they, and they alone, are right. It is not eulogy, but fact, that theirs is the path of the just, shining more and more unto the perfect day—denied only by the besotted with injustice, the committed to crime. Consider, then, not only what you owe to your slavery-encursed country, your enslaving as well as enslaved countrymen, your fathers' memory, your remotest posterity, the Christian religion, which forbids the sacrifice of one man's rights to another man's interests, and which knows no distinction of caste, color, or condition,—but consider, also, what you owe to those individuals and to that brotherhood who have battled twenty years in the breach for your freedom, involved with that of the meanest slave.

Imagine how the case stood with those who perished by suffocation in the Black Hole at Calcutta. Suppose that some of their number had felt the sublime impulse to place their bodies in the door, and the high devoted hearts to stand the crushing till dawn awoke the tyrant; the rest of that doomed band might have passed out alive. This is what the American Anti-Slavery Society has been unflinchingly doing for you, and for the rest of the nation, amid torture, insult, and curses, through a long night of terror and despair. The life of the land, its precious moral sense, has been thus kept from suffocation. The free agitating air of faithful speech has saved it.

The soul of the United States is not dead, thanks, under Providence, to that noble fellowship of resolute souls, to find whom the nation has been winnowed. Do your duty by them, in the name of self-respect. Such companionship is an honor accorded to but few, and of that worthy few I would fain count you one. Strike, then, with them at the existence of slavery, and you will see individual slaves made free, anti-slavery leaven introduced into parties and churches, instruction diffused, the products of free labor multiplied, and fugitives protected, in exact proportion to the energy of the grand onset against the civil system.

Source: Maria Weston Chapman, *"How Can I Help Abolish Slavery?" or, Counsels to the Newly Converted*. Anti-Slavery Tract No. 14 (New York: American Anti-Slavery Society, 1855).

The Next Thing to Hell (1856)

Harriet Tubman

Most abolitionists supported the Underground Railroad, the network of surreptitious routes and safe houses for runaway slaves. Some actively participated in it as "stationmasters" or "agents" by offering shelter to fugitives and arranging their transport. More served indirectly by contributing funds to help settle refugees once they arrived in a free state.

Harriet Tubman (1820/22–1913) had more hands-on experience on the Underground Railroad than any other abolitionist. Born a slave on Maryland's Eastern Shore, she escaped in 1849. Over the next decade, fueled by her intense Christian faith, she returned to Maryland again and again to lead family members and acquaintances to freedom, frequently singing spirituals about liberation to inform slaves of her presence. Her hair-raising exploits became the stuff of legend, earning her the title "Moses of her people."

Tubman never learned to read and write. But she was interviewed in 1856 while living in Canada, and was candid about her detestation of human bondage. It is, she said, the next thing to hell.

I grew up like a neglected weed—ignorant of liberty, having no experience of it. Then I was not happy or contented: every time I saw a white man I was afraid of being carried away. I had two sisters carried away in a chain-gang—one of them left two children. We were always uneasy. Now I've been free, I know what a dreadful condition slavery is. I have seen hundreds of escaped slaves, but I never saw one who was willing to go back and be a slave. I have no opportunity to see my friends in my native land. We would rather stay in our native land, if we could be as free there as we are here. I think slavery is the next thing to hell. If a person would send another into bondage, he would, it appears to me, be bad enough to send him into hell, if he could.

SOURCE: Benjamin Drew, *The Refugee: Or, the Narratives of Fugitive Slaves in Canada* (Boston: John P. Jewett and Company, 1856), 30.

Final Speech at His Trial (1859)

John Brown

In raiding the arsenal at Harpers Ferry, Virginia (now West Virginia) in October 1859, John Brown (1800–1859) hoped to use its weapons to launch a slave insurrection. He was one of the few abolitionists willing to resort to violence to end slavery, as indicated by both the raid and his participation in guerilla warfare between opponents and proponents of slavery in Bleeding Kansas three years earlier.

The raid was a dismal failure. Union troops, commanded by Colonel Robert E. Lee, quickly smashed it, killing two of Brown's sons who had participated in the raid and seriously wounding Brown himself. Captured, tried for treason, and convicted, Brown was hanged in December 1859.

In his final speech at the close of his trial, Brown rather disingenuously claims that he never intended violence. Moreover, he insists that his harsh sentence would never have been imposed had he been fighting for rich and powerful whites rather than oppressed slaves, and then justifies his action by appealing to scripture.

There's no doubt that Brown was a deeply religious man who believed that he had been commissioned by God to liberate slaves. Whether his resort to violence was an appropriate Christian response to end injustice has been debated ever since. Abolitionists of his day were torn in their responses to it.

I have, may it please the Court, a few words to say. In the first place, I deny everything but what I have already admitted, of a design on my part to free Slaves. I intended, certainly, to have made a clean thing of that matter, as I did last winter, when I went into Missouri, and there took Slaves, without the snapping of a gun on either side, moving them through the country, and finally leaving them in Canada. I desired to have done the same thing again, on a much larger scale. That was all I intended. I never did intend murder, or treason, or the destruction of property, or to excite or incite Slaves to rebellion, or to make insurrection.

I have another objection, and that is, that it is unjust that I should suffer such a penalty. Had I interfered in the manner, and which I admit has been fairly proved—for I admire the truthfulness and candor of the greater portion of the witnesses who have testified in this case,—had I so interfered in behalf of the Rich, the Powerful, the Intelligent, the so-called Great, or in behalf of any of their friends, either father, mother, brother, sister, wife, or children, or any of that class, and suffered and sacrificed what I have in this interference, it would have been all right. Every man in this Court would have deemed it an act worthy a reward, rather than a punishment.

This Court acknowledges too, as I suppose, the validity of the LAW OF GOD. I saw a book kissed, which I suppose to be the BIBLE, or at least the NEW TESTAMENT, which teaches me that, "All things whatsoever I would that men should do to me, I should do even so to them" [Matthew 7:12]. It teaches me further, to "Remember them that are in bonds, as bound with them" [Hebrews 13:3]. I endeavored to act up to that instruction. I say I am yet too young to understand that GOD is any respecter of persons. I believe that to have interfered as I have done, as I have always freely admitted I have done, in behalf of his despised poor, I have done no wrong, but RIGHT.

Now, if it is deemed necessary that I should forfeit my life, for the furtherance of the ends of justice, and MINGLE MY BLOOD FURTHER WITH THE BLOOD OF MY CHILDREN, and with the blood of millions in this Slave country, whose rights are disregarded by wicked, cruel, and unjust enactments,—I say, LET IT BE DONE.

Let me say one word further: I feel entirely satisfied with the treatment I have received on my trial. Considering all the circumstances, it has been more generous than I expected; but I feel no consciousness of guilt. I have stated from the first what was my intention, and what was not. I never had any design against the liberty of any person, nor any disposition to commit treason, or excite Slaves to rebel, or make any general insurrection. I never encouraged any man to do so, but always discouraged any idea of that kind.

Let me say something, also, in regard to the statements made by some of those who were connected with me. I hear that it has been stated by some of them, that I have induced them to join me; but the contrary is true. I do not say this to injure them, but as regarding their weakness. Not one but joined me of his own accord, and the greater part at their own expense. A number of them I never saw and never had a word of conversation with, till the day they came to me, and that was for the purpose I have stated. Now I have done.

—John Brown

SOURCE: Broadside: "ADDRESS OF JOHN BROWN to the Virginia Court, when about to receive the SENTENCE OF DEATH, For his heroic attempt at Harper's Ferry, to Give deliverance to the captives, and to let the oppressed go free." (Boston, Massachusetts, circa December 1859).

L'Envoy

Laus Deo! (1865)

John Greenleaf Whittier

Massachusetts Quaker John Greenleaf Whittier (1807–1892) had originally planned on a career in politics. But when he called for the immediate emancipation of slaves in an 1833 pamphlet, he so antagonized his state's political machine that his prospects of elected office evaporated. So he devoted himself for the next three decades to the abolitionist cause, becoming a founding member of the American Anti-Slavery Society, traveling extensively to lecture on abolitionism, and expressing in both prose and verse his opposition to human bondage.

"Laus Deo!" ("Praise God!") was inspired, Whittier tells us, when he heard the bells in his town ringing to celebrate the passage of the Thirteenth Amendment, the constitutional referendum which ended American slavery once and for all on January 31, 1865. The poem's "It is done!" conveys the sense of jubilation felt by all abolitionists when their decades-long struggle to end one of this nation's greatest injustices ended in victory.

It is done!
Clang of bell and road of gun
Send the tidings up and down.
How the belfries rock and reel,
How the great guns, peal on peal,
Fling the joy from town to town!

Ring, O bells!
Every stroke exulting tells
Of the burial hour of crime.
Loud and long, that all may hear,
Ring for every listening ear
Of Eternity and Time!

Let us kneel:
God's own voice is in that peal,
And this spot is holy ground.
Lord, forgive us! What are we,
That our eyes this glory see,
That our ears have heard the sound!

For the Lord
On the whirlwind is broad;
In the earthquake he has spoken;
He has smitten with his thunder
The iron walls asunder,
And the gates of brass are broken!

Loud and long
Lift the old exulting song,
Sing with Miriam by the sea:
He has cast the mighty down;
Horse and rider sink and drown;
He hath triumphed gloriously!

Did we dare,
In our agony of prayer,
Ask for more than he has done?
When was ever his right hand
Over any time or land
Stretched as now beneath the sun!

How they pale,
Ancient myth, and song, and tale,
In this wonder of our days,
When the cruel rod of war
Blossoms white with righteous law
And the wrath of man is praise.

Blotted out!
All within and all about
Shall a fresher life begin;
Freer breathe the universe
As it rolls its heavy curse
On the dead and buried sin.

It is done!
In the circuit of the sun
Shall the sound thereof go forth.
It shall bid the sad rejoice,
It shall give the dumb a voice,
It shall belt with joy the earth!

Ring and swing
Bells of joy! on morning's wing
Send the song of praise abroad;
With a sound of broken chains,
Tell the nations that He reigns,
Who alone is Lord and God!

SOURCE: John Greenleaf Whittier, *Poems* (New York: Thomas Y. Crowell, 1902), 422–23.

FOR FURTHER EXPLORATION

Aptheker, Herbert. *Abolitionism: A Revolutionary Movement*. Boston, MA: Twayne, 1989.

Basker, James G., ed. *American Antislavery Writings: Colonial Beginnings to Emancipation*. New York: Library of America, 2012.

Blackett, R. J. M. *Building an Antislavery Wall: Black Americans in the Atlantic Abolitionist Movement, 1830–1860*. Baton Rouge: Louisiana State University Press, 1983.

Dillon, Merton L. *The Abolitionists: The Growth of a Dissenting Minority*. New York: Norton, 1974.

Drake, Thomas E. *Quakers and Slavery in America*. New Haven, CT: Yale University Press, 1950.

Essig, James D. *The Bonds of Wickedness: American Evangelicals against Slavery, 1770–1808*. Philadelphia, PA: Temple University Press, 1982.

Filler, Louis. *The Crusade Against Slavery, 1830–1860*. New York: Harper and Row, 1960.

Goodman, Paul. *Of One Blood: Abolitionism and the Origins of Racial Equality*. Oakland: University of California Press, 1998.

Harrold, Stanley. *American Abolitionists*. New York: Pearson, 2001.

———. *The Abolitionists and the South, 1831–1861*. Lexington: University Press of Kentucky, 1995.

Jeffrey, Julie Roy. *The Great Silent Army of Abolitionists: Ordinary Women in the Antislavery Movement*. Chapel Hill: University of North Carolina Press, 1998.

Jordan, Ryan P. *Slavery and the Meetinghouse: The Quakers and the Abolitionist Dilemma, 1820–1865*. Bloomington: Indiana University Press, 2007.

Lowance, Mason, ed. *Against Slavery: An Abolitionist Reader*. New York: Penguin, 2000.

Mabee, Carlton. *Black Freedom: The Nonviolent Abolitionists from 1830 Through the Civil War*. New York: Macmillan, 1970.

McKivigan, John R. *The War Against Proslavery Religion: Abolitionism and the Northern Churches, 1830–1865*. Ithaca, NY: Cornell University Press, 1984.

McPherson, James M. *The Abolitionist Legacy*. Princeton, NJ: Princeton University Press, 1975.

Oakes, James. *Freedom National: The Destruction of Slavery in the United States, 1861–1865*. New York: Norton, 2013.

Pease, Jane H., and William H. Pease. *They Who Would Be Free: Blacks' Search for Freedom, 1830–1861*. Cambridge, MA: Athenaeum, 1974.

Perry, Lewis. *Radical Abolitionism: Anarchy and the Government of God in Antislavery Thought*. Ithaca, NY: Cornell University Press, 1973.

Quarles, Benjamin. *Black Abolitionists*. New York: Oxford University Press, 1977.

Sinha, Manisha. *The Slave's Cause: A History of Abolition*. New Haven, CT: Yale University Press, 2017.

Soderland, Jean R. *Quakers and Slavery: A Divided Spirit*. Princeton, NJ: Princeton University Press, 1985.

Speicher, Anna. *Religious World of Anti-Slavery Women: Spirituality in the Lives of Five Abolitionist Women*. Syracuse, NY: Syracuse University Press, 2000.

Stewart, James Brewer. *Holy Abolitionists: The Abolitionists and American Slavery*. New York: Hill and Wang, 1997.

Walters, Ronald G. *The Antislavery Appeal: American Abolitionism after 1830*. Baltimore, MD: Johns Hopkins University Press, 1976.

Wyatt-Brown, Bertram. *Lewis Tappan and the Evangelical War Against Slavery*. Cleveland, OH: Case Western Reserve University Press, 1969.

Yee, Shirley J. *Black Women Abolitionists: A Study in Activism, 1828–1860*. Knoxville: University of Tennessee, 1992.